BIRTHRIGHT OF FREEDOM

A Study in the Book of Judges

Doyle & Rebecca Musser

WESTBOW
PRESS®
A DIVISION OF THOMAS NELSON
& ZONDERVAN

Scripture quotations marked NASB are taken from The New American Standard Bible®, Copyright © 1960, 1962, 1963, 1968, 1971, 1972, 1973, 1975, 1977, 1995 by The Lockman Foundation. Used by permission.

Scripture quotations marked NIV are taken from The Holy Bible, New International Version®, NIV® Copyright © 1973, 1978, 1984, 2011 by Biblica, Inc.® Used by permission. All rights reserved worldwide.

Scripture quotations marked NKJV are taken from the New King James Version®. Copyright © 1982 by Thomas Nelson. Used by permission. All rights reserved.

WestBow Press books may be ordered through booksellers or by contacting:

WestBow Press
A Division of Thomas Nelson & Zondervan
1663 Liberty Drive
Bloomington, IN 47403
www.westbowpress.com
844-714-3454

Because of the dynamic nature of the Internet, any web addresses or links contained in this book may have changed since publication and may no longer be valid. The views expressed in this work are solely those of the author and do not necessarily reflect the views of the publisher, and the publisher hereby disclaims any responsibility for them.

Any people depicted in stock imagery provided by Getty Images are models, and such images are being used for illustrative purposes only. Certain stock imagery © Getty Images.

ISBN: 978-1-9736-5056-0 (sc)
ISBN: 978-1-9736-5057-7 (e)

Library of Congress Control Number: 2019900290

Print information available on the last page.

WestBow Press rev. date: 04/05/2022

Contents

Acknowledgments vii

Preface ix

Personal Introduction xiii

Introduction to This Study xv

How to Get the Most Out of This Study xvii

Chapter 1   Foundational Concepts 1

Chapter 2   Historical Foundation 12

Chapter 3   The Aramean Curse 23

Chapter 4   The Moabite Curse 34

Chapter 5   The Canaanite Curse 43

Chapter 6   The Midianite Curse 53

Chapter 7   Jotham's Curse 65

Chapter 8   The Ammonite Curse 75

Chapter 9   The Philistine Curse 86

Chapter 10 In Conclusion 97

Endnotes 103

Selected Bibliography 105

Acknowledgments

This study is the serendipitous convergence of life lessons, experiences and inspirations from so many people. To all our family, friends, teachers, co-workers, and mentors who have helped shape and grow our lives, we honor you and thank you from the bottom of our hearts.

We are particularly grateful to Arthur Burke, whose teachings on the Biblical Judges launched our own study and, to Johnny Enlow, whose book, *The Seven Mountain Prophecy*, partners with the lessons in Judges.

Elizabeth Heuer, Mom, Pastor's wife, educator, and more, thank you for a thorough line edit of the manuscript. Your eyes saw what ours could not.

Most of all, we thank our God-Father, Son, and Holy Spirit- for not leaving us stranded with all our baggage, but delivering and emancipating us in love, so we may give what we have been given.

Soli Deo Gloria!

Preface

Matthew 28:18-20

"All authority in Heaven and on earth has been given to
Me. Therefore, go and make disciples of all nations,
baptizing them in the name of the Father and of the Son
and of the Holy Spirit, and teaching them to obey everything
I have commanded you. And surely I am with you always,
to the very end of the age." (NIV)

Jesus's closing words to the disciples in the above passage launched a revolution to establish the Kingdom of God on earth. With the cross as the mechanism of sacrifice, the sinless, wounded body and blood of Jesus-Messiah completely fulfilled the just requirement of the Law of Most High God so that the love of Father-God might be requited in "whoever believes in Him. . . (Jesus, Son of God) (John 3:16b). " This was the overthrow of the usurper "who came to steal, to kill and to destroy, (John 10:10, NKJV). "The authority Christ gained has been delegated to every blood-bought believer for the advance of His Kingdom.

But "we are not just soldiers of the cross, we are heirs to the throne . . . made to be vessels of His glory and vehicles of His light."[1] Jon and Jolene Hamill have written powerfully in their book, *Crown & Throne,* "In place of the darkness and bondage of the world systems Jesus commissions transformation of individuals and nations by a spiritual revolution that empowers freedom."[2] The apostle Paul said it earlier in Galatians 5:1a (NIV), "It is for freedom Christ has set us free."

Two thousand years later, how do we fare? The reviews are mixed. China, one of the largest, most populous nations on the earth, continues to experience exponential Kingdom growth despite political oppression and persecution since the 1930's. World missions experts forecast reaching the goal of every people group having a viable fellowship of believers in Jesus by 2020. There are global prayer networks. Outbreaks of revival, accompanied by miraculous signs and wonders, are reported in various places on earth. At the same time, there are also increases in the works of darkness Jesus spoke about in Matthew 24: war, famine, persecution, hatred, betrayal, an increase of wickedness in the earth, and love-less-ness. Terrorist groups of men and women who are sold out to an agenda of violence, hatred, and death spawned from the master deceiver are at work in almost every nation. The fury of hell rages against Jerusalem, the seat of God's throne in the earth, and against the Christ-followers who also bear the authority of that throne. Truly, the darkness is getting darker but, the Light is growing brighter.

Jesus's promise, "Surely I am with you to the very end of the age (Matthew 28:20, NIV)," is both comforting and empowering. That He is with us brings confidence in the declaration of God that HE will accomplish His purposes in the earth. With Christ's presence comes the release of His mind, His strategy, and His authority to carry it out. Fresh revelation about God's commission for His people "to displace the evil principalities on the mountains (of influence in cultures) and occupy them with Kingdom citizens,"[3] is emancipating a generation to pursue God-given birthrights with passion and excellence. A greater understanding of the Courts of Heaven is producing a paradigm shift in the Body of Christ which allows the plans of God to be activated in the earth realm. We pray, "Your Kingdom come, Your will be done on earth as it is in heaven (Matthew 6:10, NIV)," and Christ's presence with us enables the Father's answer. "The crown and throne movement God is now birthing into this world is foremost a progression from slavery to freedom,"[4] and our mandate comes from Jesus's own.

Luke 4:14-21 gives the account of the launch of Jesus's public ministry. After His baptism and the testing in the wilderness, "Jesus returned to Galilee in the power of the Spirit (verse 14a, NIV)." One Sabbath He went to the synagogue, which was His custom, where He stood to read the Scripture for the day. He read from Isaiah 60:1-2, then sat back down. Imagine the pregnant silence as people fixed their eyes on Him. What would He say about what had been read? Verse 21 tells us, 'He began by saying to them, "Today this Scripture is fulfilled in your hearing."' His reading revealed five purposes for the Spirit's anointing: good news, release for captives, recovery of sight for the blind, emancipation of the down-trodden, and proclamation of the Lord's favor. This was, and is, both amazing and wonderful! The good news is most simply spoken in John 3:16. God loves us so much He willingly gave His Son to redeem us and re-establish the way to intimacy with Him. More than that, this good news returns to the believer the access to birthright and inheritance. Freedom is the focus of the next three purposes: freedom from our captivity/imprisonment, freedom from our blindness, and freedom from oppression. The apostle Paul wrote in Galatians 5:1, "It is for freedom that Christ has set us free (NIV)." As we are set free and learn to live in the way of Christ, we experience the fifth purpose, the year of the Lord's favor.

In this study we will explore seven specific areas that hold us back from the freedom God intends. After each lesson we will invite the Holy Spirit to apply the Word to our lives. Then, we will follow Kingdom protocol for dealing with any issues that affect and infect that area of our lives. May God bless each of you as you study, pray, and respond to this invitation to freedom.

Personal Introduction

Our bankruptcy was finalized in September of 2009. It was not the most positive season in our lives, at least by earthly standards; nor was it the hardest. We had lived on the edge, financially speaking, from the start of our marriage in 1974. Over the course of thirty-plus years, we had moved halfway across the country, raised eight children while living in various apartments, worked a variety of jobs, earned a Master's degree, and changed careers. All the while, we loved God as best we knew, tithed faithfully, and even served sacrificially in the local church. Through this period there were some very low times when food stamps and welfare supplemented a too meager income. Through it all the Lord never left us. In every circumstance He was faithful to heal, to teach, and to refine us, His children. When we arrived at this bankruptcy season, we knew we were safe in His hands.

The Lord actually used the bankruptcy to confront some life-long issues so that He could launch us into a new season. Early on I, Doyle, was introduced to Arthur Burke's teaching on the *Seven Curses on Your Finances*, from the book of Judges in the Bible. Listening to the CDs convicted me of six out of the seven points. I asked the team of prayer ministers who were helping me to work through issues related to bankruptcy to listen to the CDs and pray about them with me, which they willingly did. Becky subsequently listened and prayed the prayers and renunciations too. Before long, we found ourselves sharing our personal revolution with friends who also needed "something." That was God's kick-off.

However, this was not to be a new game, just the second half. Over the years the Lord had sown all kinds of dream-seeds in our hearts. The very first followed our year as house parents at a residential treatment facility. We left that position with a deep desire to someday have a home-based ministry where we could again work together. Many other ideas came in the seasons of the Lord teaching, refining, and using us. We often mistook these for wishful ideas because lack of money was our limiting factor. Yet, they did not just fade and die. More and more ideas came as the years passed.

During the early months after the bankruptcy and the deliverance from the "curses," we seized an opportunity to take a class on entrepreneurism. Assignments to write out our dreams, speak them aloud, and pray about them activated a deep place in both of us. Possibility and hope floated free from the old constraints. The convergence of this new freedom with all our education, experience, the awakening of dreams, encouragement of others, and time, opened the door for us to think about ministry—that first dream in our marriage.

The next step came when we were invited to teach on the seven curses material at the House of Prayer in Hartford, CT. God made it clear from the outset that we were not to puppet Arthur Burke. We were to teach out of our own training and understanding of Scripture and experiences on the paths God had led us down. While we realized the importance of learning from the revelation others had received, everything needs to be tested, so the lectures became a Bible study course. One of the early study groups proposed a name change because they realized that the freedom gained was much greater than the curses, hence the name, Birthright of Freedom. The Holy Spirit continues to open the truth of the history of Judges and its applications for us today.

Harbor Shalom, Inc. was formed in 2011 as a 501(c) 3 public nonprofit corporation. As we believe God for the dreams and destiny He is bringing forth, we are excited to witness the freedom released in those who take this class. May you be blessed, as we have been, by the Birthright of Freedom (Galatians 5:1).

Introduction to This Study

Birthright of Freedom may be the most unusual Bible study you have ever embarked upon. We hope so! You should know from the outset that it is not a scholarly treatise from academia. Nor is it a feel-good-quick-fix for the harsh realities of life. There is no special knowledge accessible to only a select few. No, instead, out of the riches of His grace, God is opening a greater understanding of His Word in order to better equip the people of God for Christ's return.

Though the primary scripture focus is the book of Judges, Israel and every one of her oppressors has a back story which the student will explore, along with New Testament applications and a Jesus-antidote. (Seven miracles in the Gospel of John provide an excellent context for these.) Daily Bible readings and thought questions will lend structure for the journey. At the end of each teaching is a prayer for freedom from the chapter's particular oppression. We believe Paul's declaration in 2 Timothy 3:16-17, "All Scripture is inspired by God and profitable for teaching, for reproof, for correction, for training in righteousness; that the man of God may be adequate, equipped for every good work (NASB)." Furthermore, the Holy Spirit is fully capable of bringing truth, revelation, understanding, and application to each believing student. Always the litmus test is: Is it true? Then, is it life-giving? Does it glorify God alone? At the end of the day, is one freer to love God, obey Him, and walk in authority in the sphere that is one's unique birthright?

There are several key concepts that are woven throughout this study. It seems prudent to identify them here so that we begin with a common understanding of their use in this context.

- Birthright: According to Webster's Dictionary, birthright is "any right of privilege to which a person is entitled by birth."[5] The birthright for the seed of Abraham was both physical, the family blessings and land, and spiritual, as the covenant people of God. Followers of Jesus are adopted into the seed of Abraham with all the rights, privileges and responsibilities—except land.

- Freedom: Fundamentally, freedom is the state of being at liberty to choose. From God's perspective, freedom may be like a two-sided coin. There is freedom from the curse and bondage of sin in all its aspects, and there is freedom to be and do all that our loving Creator designed for us before we were even born.

- Inheritance: Though we tend to think of inheritance in terms of money, it is that which is received or earned by one generation and passed on to the next to be built upon. When the Israelites came into their promised land, God made specific allocations of property to each of the twelve tribes, except the Levites, which were to remain as a perpetual inheritance to every generation. Provisions were made for the return of "lost" property to the lawful heirs in the year of Jubilee. This was a tangible demonstration of an even greater spiritual inheritance which God's people were to pass on.

- Covenant: A covenant is a binding agreement between two parties, established by blood sacrifice, enforced by honor, and dissolved only by death; it is the mode of relationship between God and His people, both in the Old Testament—established first with Adam—and in the New Testament—completed in Jesus Christ. Gratitude, honor, obedience, and worship (intimacy), are the means of living out covenant with God.

- Generational sin: Generational sins are patterns of un-repentant sin, or iniquity, repeated generation after generation in a family, people group, or nation, whose consequences bring bondage and hindrances to the liberty and fruitfulness God intends.

How to Get the Most Out of This Study

1. Mindset. 2 Timothy 2:15 (NKJV) says, "Be diligent to present yourself to God, a worker who does not need to be ashamed, rightly dividing the word of truth." If you study the context of this verse, Paul is encouraging Timothy to have the right mindset. Be a good soldier; be strong in grace; suffer hardship; be faithful; don't get entangled with everyday affairs; be hard working; run hard for the prize; endure all things; be grounded in the Word of God. Why? To become a vessel of gold and silver, useful to the Master. So, set your mind to study diligently and effectively.

2. Preparation. There are Scripture readings and thought questions for each day of the week. These will pertain to the lesson. In addition, there is some more expository reading, with questions embedded, which will help to develop the perspective and focus for the central passage in Judges. It is important to have read, studied, prayed, and thought through these before class.

3. Pray. Pray. Pray. For some of you this study will present a huge battle. Even in getting started, many will find that all kinds of obstacles suddenly begin appearing. Pray for God to help you press through. Pray for the Holy Spirit to come and lead you into the truth, for He will open your eyes and heart to see what is in the Word for you.

4. The prayers of renunciation, cleansing, and release at the end of each chapter, three through nine, are not a formula. However, they are crafted to cover important details relative to the chapter focus. You may pray your own prayer, but we advise two things: (1) incorporate all significant aspects as in the prepared prayer, and (2) pray aloud as a declaration.

CHAPTER 1
Foundational Concepts
Weekly Readings

Day 1: Read Galatians 5:1.

What are two important ideas you see in this verse?

What are two things this verse tells us to do?

Day 2: Read James 5:13–16.

How is healing connected with being in community?

What other ideas do you discover in these verses?

Day 3: Read Proverbs 13:22.

What does a good man do?

What besides wealth or possessions might one inherit?

Day 4: Read Ephesians 1:1–14 and Colossians 1:9–23.

What do these passages describe as our inheritance?

Do you think inheritance is important to God?

Day 5: Read Exodus 20:1–17.

Verses 5 and 6 make a powerful statement about generational influences. What do they tell you? *What does it mean?*

Day 6: Read Romans 12:1–2 and 1 Corinthians 13:11.

What does each passage tell you and how are they linked?

Key Verse: Galatians 5:1 (NASB)

It is for freedom that Christ set us free, therefore keep standing firm and do not be subject again to a yoke of slavery.

This is so awesome! When it actually penetrates mind and spirit, this truth can overwhelm us. God so loved us that He gave His only Son (John 3:16, NASB). Our Abba Father wants freedom for us, even more than we want it ourselves. Too often we think of our God as a tyrant or harsh task master. *Abba* is a term of endearment, of intimacy. He loves us so much He wants the very best for us.

The rest of the verse is just as important as the first part. It is so easy to lose freedom. We need to keep standing firm, (How do we do that?) and not let ourselves be subject again to a yoke of slavery. We are to help each other, be transparent, and pray for each other. We are to learn to walk by the Spirit and cooperate in His transformation process. In our own lives, we have seen how the weight of the baggage from the past—ours and our ancestors—can affect our existence. Getting rid of that baggage is liberating indeed!

Our first goal is to explore together some of the ways we can be yoked into slavery. Then we want to pray together to get rid of that baggage. As we offload the burdens of generational consequences, we will be able to recognize more fully the freedom we have in Christ.

The second major goal is to explore inheritance. We have come to understand that inheritance is very important to our Abba Father. If you have read through the accounts of the Israelite journey from Egypt to the Promised Land, you will remember that the Lord gave each family its own inheritance. Not only that, but the system that God set up required that should land be sold or given over for any reason, it was to be returned to the rightful heir in the year of Jubilee. Scripture teaches in Proverbs 13:22 (NIV), "A good man leaves an inheritance to his children's children." As we are looking at generational curses and blessings this obligation is very important. It begs the questions, What are we inheriting from our ancestors? What are we passing on?" There are, of course, tangible things like land, houses, and money. There are physical characteristics like skin, eye, and hair color, predisposition to diseases, and mental illness in our family lines. Have you considered that there might be spiritual and intangible characteristics that have been passed down?

Ephesians 2:10 (NASB) tells us that, "We are His workmanship, created in Christ Jesus for good works, which God prepared beforehand, that we should walk in them." This speaks of birthright. This includes the destiny and purpose God has planned for us; it will draw on the inheritance we receive. Like our physical inheritance, we are safe to assume that this also comes to us through our bloodlines—fathers and mothers to sons and daughters.

World View

Did you ever consider the possibility that no one else in the whole world thinks exactly like you do? No one else, except an identical twin, has your genetic makeup. No one else, even your identical twin, will experience life in the same place, time, conditions, or quality as you. From birth every child has already begun the process of learning what life is all about. As children grow, circumstances and experiences will develop that matrix, or grid, by which they can interpret life in the world, and out of which they will respond. This is *world view*.

Chris Vallotton, in *Supernatural Ways of Royalty*, speaks about this world view concept in terms of core values—"the lenses that determine the way we see life. They are the interpreters of our world."[6]

Another way to think about the factors that create this strategic framework is what John Eldredge, in *Wild at Heart*, describes as a "wound-message-vow-cycle."[7] Wounds from significant, powerful people in our lives send messages to our souls about who we are in the world. The messages prompt responses, or decisions, that we, as children, make in order to establish some kind of order or equilibrium. Subsequent events then get routed through the decisions that we made. Whether we call it a grid, core values, a cycle, or any other term, we are talking about world view. Each person has one. Always, it is learned.

Let's just think for a few minutes about the kinds of factors that shape a worldview. The time in which one lives (in war or peace, in plenty or poverty, the best of times or the worst of times), and the geographical location (mountains, valleys, cities, seacoasts, deserts, swamps), all have broad general impact on the exposure and experiences of life.

Religions all attempt to provide a framework to interpret life by creating a value system and code of behaviors relative to that frame. They are more formal strategies to impose a worldview. Even in Judaism, the God of Torah chose a people to be identified with Himself; He gave them laws and rules to live by and a place to inhabit. Revelation of God's names, God's ways, God's promises, and purposes for Israel and the whole earth are meant to provide His people with a life-giving worldview.

One's particular physical attributes in the context of contemporary culture invite powerful messages about the world. For example, a female baby born into a culture that prizes sons above daughters automatically has a strong negative to navigate through life. That is fairly easy to see. What of the more nebulous values a family or society attributes to ideas of beauty, strength, longevity, speed, agility, or intelligence? Each of us may be able to recognize some ways that those external factors have acted on our perceptions of ourselves or the world around us. Often we do not even think about them.

However, the single most important factor in the child's development of world view can be summed up in a word: relationships. Every baby, from the moment of conception, is in relationship with the mother-host. He (or she) will be affected by everything that involves his mother. He (or she) will come to respond to mother stimuli, then other non-mother stimuli as she develops in the womb, and when he is born, the mother and others who care for him will have the greatest impact on how his earliest needs are met and, therefore, on how his most fundamental questions about life are answered. Am I wanted? Is it safe? Is there enough? These are perhaps the first questions.

Since every child is thus affected by imperfect adults who were also raised up in an imperfect world by imperfect people, it is ridiculous to imagine that the messages impressed upon the child will always be true or helpful or even just benign. Because we are inherently relational, messages require responses or choices. Choices have consequences that affect subsequent circumstances and reinforce or refute the messages that set the first bars of the grid of life in position. Behavior sciences assure us that by the time a child is seven or eight years old, his or her world view is strongly set. After that time it is difficult to make significant changes in the ways a person will relate to the people and circumstances in the world.

As parents, it is sobering to think about the impact of our worldview upon our children. It requires a recognition of the grid through which we see and interpret our own lives. That in itself seems to demand a full disclosure of our past as well as our parents' input from their worldview. How much of what I have come to believe was passed down to me? How much of that was re-interpreted through my own circumstances, perceptions, and choices? Who can accomplish such a thing? World view is fundamental; God has made provision for reclaiming and correcting each person's. That provision is a process with an old-fashioned name: sanctification.

Romans 12:1–2 directs us to submit ourselves to God and to the Holy Spirit's transforming work for the renewing of our minds. The Holy Spirit can and will inform us, teach us truth, apply that truth, and bring about transformation as we bring all of our past, all of our present, and all of our future into submission to God. That is part of the Apostle Paul's declaration in Ephesians 2:8–10.

As our worldview yields to God's view, the blessings of holy birthright, inheritance, and destiny will be formed in and through us. Lest we think that this is optional, the scriptures are careful to exhort us "as obedient children, not conforming yourselves to the former lusts, as in your ignorance; but as He who called you is holy, you also be holy in all your conduct (1 Peter 1:13–14, NKJV)." Finally, the writer of Hebrews instructs us in Hebrews 12:14 (NASB) to "pursue peace with all people, and the sanctification without which no one will see the Lord."

Attitude

Have you heard the saying, "Attitude determines altitude?" Many motivational seminars will throw around statements such as this. While there is some truth to them, let's be clear about their foundation. These motivational tools are all about self-improvement or self-advancement. Their intent is to better oneself, to have more, to earn more, to become more in the current culture's estimation. If we are to have a world view aligned with Jesus, then we need to know what Jesus would do. Take a look at the following scriptures. Then, write down in your own words what they say to you.

- Micah 6:8
- Matthew 6:31–34
- Philippians 2:5–13
- 1 Peter 5:5–11

All four of these passages, just a sampling from many, are exhortations to right attitude. In Genesis 29:31–35 we have another example of the impact of attitude. Let's explore this account together.

Jacob had married Leah, a trick of her father Laban's, without loving her. Days later, Rachel, the desired bride, was wed to Jacob as well. It does not take much imagination to determine that Leah must have felt unwanted. Genesis 29:31 tells us that God saw this miserable situation and opened Leah's womb. God honored Leah. But when Reuben was born, Leah wanted her husband's blessing. Though Leah conceived three more times, her goal was to secure Jacob's love and favor. Until the fourth son, Judah, was born, Leah's focus and attitude were on obtaining the impossible from Jacob while disregarding the true source of unfailing love and blessing. Judah's birth came with a change of mind: verse 35, "This time I will praise the Lord." Judah's name means praise. Out of Judah's lineage came King David, Davidic worship, and the promised Messiah, Jesus.

Motivation and attitude flow together. The pursuit of Truth, birthright, or freedom cannot legitimately be simply to pacify our lusts. As we venture into this study of Israel in the time of the Judges we need to be clear: this is not a magic wand. Setting aside the sin that entangles us and the iniquity in our bloodlines that weighs us down and keeps us from our full inheritance is essential to appropriating God's purposes which were sown into our lives before we were even born. Attitude is the only thing you really have control over, so choose a good one. Embrace the mindset in the Scriptures reviewed previously. Reach in to your birthright of freedom.

A Look at Curses

What do you think of when you hear the word curse? Perhaps you immediately think of swearing or speaking the Lord's name inappropriately. That dates us, doesn't it? Or perhaps you see it as a confrontation where, in anger, one party shouts, "Curse you." You may sometimes hear a tale of a series of tragic events, the conclusion of which is, "They must be under some kind of curse." You may remember stories or movies where one person put a curse on another through an incantation, ritual, or spell. Are any or all of these curses? What does the Bible say about curses?

The Bible identifies five specific types of curses.

1. The curse of our own sin: We do not often think in terms of a curse when we think of sin. Genesis 3:13–19 records the curses that God spoke in judgment of Adam and Eve, the serpent, and the entire created world for that first sin. Romans 6:23, "For the wages of sin is death. . ." tells us that when we sin we are under the wrath and judgment of God, *i.e.*, under sin's curse. Hallelujah! There is a remedy: Christ bore our curse on the cross (Galatians 3:13-14).

2. Word Curses: These are negative words spoken to us, about us, or even by us, which become barriers to our God given potential. Proverbs tells us that the words we speak have the power of life or death. (Proverbs 12:18; 13:2; 15:1–2 are just a few examples.) Think about it, God spoke the universe into existence. He created man in His image and gave him dominion over the earth. Consider Jabez in the Bible. He asked God to change his name because it was a constant, inescapable declaration that he had brought pain to his mother. Names have power. Perhaps you remember the childish ditty, *"Sticks and stones may break my bones, but words can never hurt me."* Rubbish! Words spoken and **absorbed** can do more damage than sticks and stones. Comments like "You are so stupid." or "You'll never amount to anything." or "Nothing you have to say matters." or "You are just like your _____." are all statements that demean and curse, or constrain, a person, especially a child. Proverbs 3:27 tells us that what we hear becomes what we think. What we think we will then become. Negative words can be a powerful curse.

3. Curse of broken vows and/or judgments: In the Scriptures, vows are primarily words spoken that obligate the speaker to someone or some course of action. Repeatedly the Psalmists declares, "I will fulfill my vows." Elsewhere he rehearses the blessing of God on the person who fulfills his vows even at cost to himself (See Psalm 16). Marriage vows made by both the man and the woman commit their love, resources, honor, and obedience to each other for as long as they both live. Our experience and observation is that God honors those marriage vows made in sincerity and kept diligently, sometimes more than the couple who made them. But, in Matthew 5:33–37, Jesus warns us not to make vows or use a vow or oath to validate a statement. We are to let yes mean yes, or no mean no, period. He warns that broken vows have dire consequences. Divorce, which God hates, Malachi 2:15–16, is the breaking of

covenant vows. While Jesus explained that God made provision for divorce because of the brokenness of sinful man, He also made it clear that it brings judgment and makes families vulnerable to curses. We can see it in our society, poverty, abuse, neglect, fatherlessness, etc.…

Judgments that we make about people can also bring a curse. Jesus said in Matthew 7:1–2, "Judge not lest you be judged, for with the measure you use, the same shall be done to you." The judgment itself becomes a curse. How? Have you ever heard someone say, "I will never be like my father."? Most often the very thing those words were judging becomes their own sin.

4. Curses of witchcraft/occult: Tapping into occult power to manipulate people or circumstances through rituals, spells, hexes, or incantations is cursing. All of these are part of the detestable things that God forbade His people to do (Deuteronomy 18:10–12). Engaging in the cursing of witchcraft releases demonic power to harm. Though participants do it to access power, such control is a deception that brings bondage and all of it falls under God's judgment.

5. Generational curses: Exodus 20:5 says that the sins of a father are passed on to his children and grandchildren to the third and fourth generation. Unless sin is confessed, repented of, and covered by the blood of atonement, Jesus's blood, its stain remains. Satan, the Accuser before the throne of God, will use it against any person in the bloodline for as long as it is uncontested. (This is the sin and the resultant curses that we want to deal with in this study.) Generally, our first reaction to the passage in Exodus is shock. Why would a loving God perpetuate sin from generation to generation? Where is the forgiveness? The issue is unrepentance. As we worked in social work we saw in the records of our clients the perpetuation of brokenness from grandparents' wrong choices, to parents' same wrong choices, to their children's wrong choices that landed them in "residential treatment". The generational curse in this context looks like natural consequences. However, as we noted above, sin has spiritual consequences. Until the sin is dealt with, the variety of vile oppressions our adversary can use against us remains unchecked.[8]

One Thing More, No, Two

Several years ago our pastor loaned us Johnny Enlow's book, *The Seven Mountain Prophecy*. While we do not intend to regurgitate the whole revelation God gave Mr. Enlow, there are a few points it is well to carry forward in our study of Judges. Remember that God told the children of Israel that there were seven nations mightier and greater than they whom they were to annihilate. God's judgment would be released from heaven to help them. Then, Israel was to occupy the land and fully develop all its rich resources for the glory of God in the earth. God revealed to Enlow that the characteristics of these seven nations align with the seven mountains of influence attributed to each of those seven nations. It was Israel's task to live out Godly influence in the culture. Mr. Enlow contends that "the taking of the Promised Land is to be prophetically applied to our generation (Is 12:2–3)." At this time, God will exalt those who are willing to believe Him for the impossible, and nations will flow to God's Kingdom saying, "Teach us His ways."[9] It is important that God's blood bought people realize that it has always been His will for us to be at the top of the mountain in a place of pre-eminence and blessing. He has always sought to motivate us with a promised land of unlimited abundance—body, soul and spirit."[10] This is nothing less than a spiritual revolution that begins in the Church of Jesus Christ and impacts individuals, cultures, nations, and the world.

Secondly, when we look at Jesus's explanations for what He did and why He did what He did, we must recognize that He lived as a man under a clear mandate from Father God to establish the Kingdom in the earth realm. We read that (Jesus) "learned obedience through the things He suffered (Hebrews 5:8 NIV)." That obedience gave Him a crown of unparalleled glory. As with the Heir, so with the co-heirs of Christ. Jon and Jolene Hamill have released the language of that mandate for us in this generation. The crown and throne mandate is that each of us:

> "Establish covenant with Christ apart from idolatry, and steward your authority to empower His justice and freedom in your sphere."[11]

This is the heart cry of Birthright of Freedom.

Prayer

ABBA FATHER, You are holy and worthy of all of my worship. That worship, described in Romans 12:1, is to give you my whole life, a living sacrifice.

By Your Spirit help me die to myself and yield all—heart, soul, mind and strength—to You. Expose to the light the hurts and subsequent choices I made which keep me from walking in intimacy with You. I want to walk in the Light, as You are the Light. Help me to bend to Your yoke Jesus, and keep my eyes on You, not on the storms around me. Grow in me the fruit of the Spirit so that I will be mature and well-grounded in spiritual sight and understanding. I do not want to be tossed about by the waves of circumstance.

Holy Spirit, I thank You for coming willingly from the Father to be my teacher, counselor, comforter, and guide. I welcome Your ministry to me. Today, I declare again my glad surrender to Your work in me, and I rejoice in the certainty that what You have begun in me, You will carry on to completion. Thank you.

May all glory, honor, dominion, power, and praise be lavished upon You, my God and Sovereign. Blessed be the Name of the LORD. Amen and amen.

CHAPTER 2
Historical Foundation
Weekly Readings

Day 1: Read Genesis 3.

What takes place in this chapter?

Day 2: Read Genesis 12:1–7 and 28:10–22.

Notice the similarities in God's visitation to Abram, and later, to Jacob.

What are all the promises God makes to each?

Day 3: Read Exodus, 20:1–21. These are the Ten Commandments.

Note verse 5. It is a key to our study.

What is God saying?

Verses 18–21. Record the peoples' response to this presentation of the Law. What do you see happening?

Why do you suppose this is significant?

Day 4: Read Deuteronomy 7, 12:28–32, 20:16–18, any one chapter of 27–30, and 30:11–16. This is lots of OT, but worth the investment of time. Look for the warnings, the commands, and the promises God repeats.

Summarize your findings/responses.

Day 5: Read Judges 1:1–3:5.

How does Israel begin in the new land?

What cycle do they quickly fall into relative to all the Deuteronomy passages read yesterday?

Day 6: Read Matthew 5:13–20 and John 5:39.

How do the ideas in these two passages connect with the other readings this week?

The Role of the Bible

What is the Bible? Is it just a bunch of stories? Is it just myths? Is it a document written by a religious group to keep people under control? Is it a code of moral guidelines? Is it history? Is it God's Holy word? If you believe it is God's words, do you think it is fabrication to make a point, allegory, or real events? Do you think it was just written by people, or do you think it originated from God as communicated by the Spirit of God?

These are basic questions with which we must wrestle in order to come to an understanding of the God of the Bible and our relationship to Him. Some of you may have thought through these things. Others may have thought, "Why bother?" We explored the concept of worldview in the last chapter, so perhaps one good answer to the why-bother-question is that it will determine whether we view life correctly or incorrectly. Jesus said, "I am the Way, and the Truth, and the Life; no one comes to the Father except through Me (John 14:6, NIV)."

Previously, we suggested that we need to have a Jesus world view even more than a Biblical world view. In the scripture passages for this week we see that Jesus did not come to abolish the Law, but to fulfill it. He said that if anyone were to add to or take from away any of the Scripture God gave, that person would be held accountable. He also said that people search the scriptures to find salvation when it is these scriptures which point to Jesus, see John 5:39.

Did you ever consider the Bible to be a love letter? It is the account of God creating a universe that is beautiful and good. God wanted someone to share it with, so He created man in His image. Adam and Eve messed up (*i.e.*, sinned), and the relationship changed fundamentally. The consequence of their sin gave dominion of this world to an arch enemy. The implications of choices and consequences in a perfect Eden were very different after Eve and Adam ate the forbidden fruit. No longer was Creator God the sole authority in the earth. They had listened to another voice, a rebellious and enticing one. They had embraced the insinuation that God had deceived them in order to confine them to less than god-ness. A seemingly simple disobedience had turned their affections away from the One Who created and loved them, gave them purpose and value, and had entrusted this magnificent creation to their dominion and stewardship. It brought shame, fear, accusation, separation, and war into the perfect world.

But God, in His unbelievable love, set a plan into motion to bring about the redemption of all His people. Just as we give guidelines and set boundaries for our children, God set boundaries. We find them in the Bible. He said that if we obey Him there will be blessing. Disobedience will bring curses. There are consequences for all we do! Just like human parents, God wants us to choose that which leads to the best life. The Bible gives us a history of the plan worked out through a man named Abram and his descendants; through kings and prophets, poets, harlots, angels, and enemies; then ultimately through Jesus Christ, the incarnation of God, Who finished God's redemptive purpose on a cruel cross. In the history is a mysterious, majestic, sometimes intimate, revelation of this supremely amazing God above all gods. The Bible also provides hope in the promises yet to be fulfilled, hope for the times in which we live, and courage to live between the two. It itself is part of God's plan.

At this juncture in the Birthright of Freedom study, we will explore briefly the scriptures preceding the book of Judges. This will give us a rudimentary glimpse at God's plan, as well as the many complications which challenged it between Genesis 1 and Judges 3. We need to study this love letter. The understanding it provides will lead us to the revelation that we, as well as Israel, need to attain our birthright and freedom.

Historical Overview Preceding Judges

The daily readings for this week highlight the history of Israel up to the time of the Judges. Judges will be the focus of our study for the remainder of this course. We take the time for this preparatory review for the same reason sages throughout the ages have warned that those who despise history are destined to repeat it. The truth is, some of history—the holy, righteous, and just portions—need to be preserved and repeated. It is the mistakes, the unholy, unrighteous, and unjust, that we need to heed and take steps to not repeat. With that in mind, let's look at the readings specified for this week.

- Genesis 3: Details the fall of Adam and Eve into sin
  1. Deceived
  2. Chose to disobey
  3. Resulting curses: serpent is to be despised; woman to have greater pain in childbearing and be subject to her husband; man's labors to be a painful toil all his life; removed from the Garden of Eden.

- Genesis 12: God separates out from the nations a people for Himself
  1. Abram is instructed to move.
  2. God promises, *"and all peoples on earth will be blessed through you"*
  3. God promises land to Abram.

- Genesis 23: Jacob's encounter with God
  1. Dream
  2. Promise renewed: *"All peoples on earth will be blessed through you and your offspring. I am with you and will watch over you wherever you go, and I will bring you back to this land."*

- Exodus 20: God gives Moses the commandments, laws, and conditions of relationship.
  1. Ten Commandments
  2. People respond by distancing themselves; Moses serves as the go-between.

- Deuteronomy 7: Receiving the Promised Land
  1. The clear, straightforward mandate: *"and when the LORD your God has delivered them over to you and you have defeated them, then you must destroy them totally. Make no treaty with them, and show them no mercy. . ."*

2. God's reason: *"For you are a people holy to the LORD your God. The LORD your God has chosen you out of all the peoples on the face of the earth to be His people, His treasured possession."*

3. God's qualifications: *"Know therefore that the LORD your God is God; He is the faithful God, keeping His covenant of love to a thousand generations of those who love Him and keep His commands. But those who hate Him He will repay to their face by destruction."*

4. How to do it: Do not be afraid of the enemies you are sent to conquer and destroy. Fear God.

- Deuteronomy 12: Restating the instructions
  1. Be careful to obey.
  2. When God brings success, be careful not to be ensnared by the false religions.

- Deuteronomy 20: REPEAT.
  1. Utterly destroy.
  2. Warning: *"Otherwise they will teach you to follow all the detestable things they do in worshiping their gods, and you will sin…*

- Deuteronomy 27 through 31:13: Moses's final instructions
  1. Mount Ebal: build an acceptable altar, set up stones with the Law carved in them, and declare the curses God has spoken for disobedience to all the laws and precepts given through Moses.
  2. Mount Gerazim: build an acceptable altar and pronounce from there all the blessings for obedience to God's laws and precepts.
     - Set you high above all nations
     - In city and country,
     - Fruitful in offspring, crops, herds, and flocks,
     - Full basket and kneading trough,
     - In all your coming and going,
     - Enemies defeated,
     - Established as God's holy people—open heavens, head-not-tail.
  3. Ending reminder: *"The secret things belong to the LORD our God, but the things revealed belong to us and to our children forever, that we may follow all the words of this Law (Deuteronomy 29:29, NIV)."*

- Judges 1:1–3:5. A funny thing happened on the way to "forever"
  1. 1:1–26 things started out well
  2. Verse 27: But Manasseh did not drive out the people. . .nor did Ephraim. . .Neither did Zebulun. . .Nor did Asher drive out those living…
  3. Chapter 2: the Angel of the Lord confronts Israel for their disobedience, "*Why have you done this? Now therefore I tell you that I will not drive them out before you; they will be thorns in your sides and their gods will be a snare to you (verse 2b, NIV).*"
  4. The generation after Joshua and all those who had witnessed God's wonders neither knew the LORD nor what He had done for Israel.
     God was very angry with Israel for their stubborn, evil ways.

Seven Mountains & Other Sevens

Earlier we introduced Johnny Enlow and *The Seven Mountain Prophecy*. Having reviewed the Biblical narrative prior to Judges, it seems beneficial to interject some thoughts from Enlow's revelation that strongly connect to the account in Judges.

First, let's look at the mountains. They are the seven major influencers of any culture or society. We have looked at the idea of world view. That connects to these mountains of influence because they have affected our parents, their parents, and on and on. How we were raised in the context of the society of our time, and our response to that milieu, help mold our world view. Here are the seven mountains Enlow identifies:

- Media
- Government
- Education
- Economy
- Religion
- Celebration (A & E)
- Family[12]

How is this connected to Judges? In your reading for this week you read Deuteronomy 7. God warned the Israelites that there were seven nations in the Promised Land who were mightier and stronger than themselves. They were not to be afraid to go into the land, and they needed to remove those nations as specifically instructed by God. According to Enlow, the characteristics of each of those nations lined up with a mountain of influence, only in the negative ways described in Scripture. They were to be removed so that they could not be a destructive influence on Israel. Israel was to be a holy people, set apart for God's purpose. They were to show the world the Kingdom of God. Those negative influences would be a thorn in their sides and distract them from their destiny. The seven nations in Deuteronomy 7 are:

- Hittites
- Girgashites
- Amorites
- Canaanites
- Perizzites
- Hivites
- Jebusites

One more "seven" to look into is found in Revelation 5. There the Apostle John writes of a vision wherein a mighty angel is looking for someone to open the Scroll. The Lion of the tribe of Judah, the Lamb who was slain, comes forward, and He is worthy to open the Scroll. Notice what is said about Him in verse 12, *"Worthy is the Lamb that was slain to receive power, and riches, and wisdom, and strength, and honor, and glory, and blessing (NIV)."* Let's think about those attributes in terms of the mountains of influence.

- Power speaks of governmental authority,
- Riches speaks of economy,
- Wisdom speaks of education,
- Strength speaks of family,
- Honor speaks of religion,
- Glory speaks of celebration,
- Blessing speaks of media.

From whom will Jesus receive these?

Another thought to ponder, if Israel was to be holy, what should the Church, the Bride of Christ, be? Remember we are grafted into the Vine (See John 15). If Israel was to remove the negative influences around them so that God could establish His kingdom on earth, what should the Body of Christ be doing in this world? True, we do not have an assignment to war against people and nations. Paul wrote to the Corinthian believers that our war is not against people (II Corinthians 10:3–6), but spiritual strongholds, arguments, and powers that war against the knowledge of God. What did Jesus tell us in Matthew 28:18–20? The idea that we are to carry this news of the Kingdom of God everywhere we go, establishing outposts or lighthouses for the Kingdom, is not a pretty philosophy. It is part of what Paul exhorted in Romans 12—being living sacrifices, being transformed by the renewing of our minds, then spreading transformation always and everywhere. God wants to take all the gifts, anointings, and talents sown into our lives and grow us into places of leadership and influence in the sphere where we are uniquely called. The Church in western culture has behaved more like apostate Israel than the apostolic church that launched at Pentecost. We have let the enemy have leadership and influence. It is time to apply due diligence to the sanctification process (Holy Spirit cleansing, correcting, renewing, teaching, etc.), so that we can actually take hold of the birthright God intends and live in fruitful freedom. Think about it!

Negative Cycles / Natural Consequences

Judges 2:6–3:5; Romans 1

"Four Score and seven years ago our fathers brought forth on this continent a new nation, conceived in Liberty and dedicated to the proposition that all men are created equal."[13] Abraham Lincoln spoke those words at a time of great brokenness and peril in the USA. That country was formed in the context of a Biblical understanding and a fundamental belief in God. Did you ever wonder how many nations were formed in covenant with God? God initiated covenant with Israel. Godly Pilgrims made covenant with God for what became the United States of America. What are the ramifications of covenant for Israel, for the USA, for any people? What might be the evidence of failure to fulfill the human side of the bargain? Think about the US or your country.

Looking at Romans 1, what do you notice that may be relevant to where you find yourself in the context of your society?

Then, look for similarities between what Paul wrote in Romans 1 and what you read in the Judges 2:6–3:5 passage.

Amazing, is it not?

As we study through Judges in the next several weeks, notice the decline in the people, both individually and culturally. Notice the resulting behaviors, relationships with God and people, and changes in the way people thought. The absolute bottom of the barrel for Israel actually comes on the heels of Judges with the prophet Samuel. As the nation declined the priesthood was corrupted, and soon, the people cried out for a king, like other nations around them. Samuel despaired at this proposition and warned of the impact of such a course of action. However, God consented to the request, explaining to Samuel that Israel's rejection was not of his leadership, but a rejection of God's sovereignty. Every step away from the authority of God, from Eden, to Mount Sinai, to the judges, to a human scepter, had consequences for Israel. How do we avoid such a cycle of decline? Where might it be at work in your life?

Footholds/What Gives Satan the Legal Right?

Ephesians 4:26–27 says, *"Be angry and yet do not sin, do not let the sun go down on your anger, and do not give the devil a foothold (NASB)."* We need to understand that any sin gives our enemy the legal right to access us. If sin is not dealt with right away, before the sun sets, submitted in repentance under the blood of Jesus before the Throne of Grace (Hebrews 4), it can become a place of regular or habitual access by our adversary—a foothold. Unconfessed, unrepentant sin, especially where some aspect of covenant has been violated, is passed in the bloodline and leaves opening for Satan's activities: to steal, to kill, and to destroy. Remember Exodus 20:4–5. Those sins, which are usually unknown to us, can be presented in the courts of heaven, as testimony against us. Until we answer the charges against us, and bring them under the authority of the blood of Jesus by confession and repentance, they give Satan a legal right to oppose us and the purposes of God in our lives. (There is a whole lot more to this idea than we can explore here. For a clear and more comprehensive understanding, go to Robert Henderson's teaching, *Operating in the Courts of Heaven.)* Therefore, we must deal with our sin conscientiously, and we must submit ourselves to the Lord for the cleansing of our bloodline, in order to actually become the people of destiny Jesus calls us to be—*"a chosen generation, a royal priesthood, a holy nation, His own special people, that you may proclaim the praises of Him who called you out of darkness into His marvelous light (1 Peter 2:9, NKJV)."*

As we work through Judges, one question that comes up is, "Where is the curse coming from?" Simply put, it comes down through the people group that is oppressing the Israelites at that particular time. Israel's own sin opened the door, but it is the oppressors' own generational sin which carries the curse. That is why the nature of the oppression is unique with each of the judges. As you read and study, make note of the differences. We will look back at origins to see how each curse began.

To review, let's look at the sequence for Israel in Judges 3:3. First, Israel disobeyed God in not removing the seven nations completely. God then allowed five nations to remain to test them. Only one of the five tormentors was part of the original seven assigned for removal. Remember the angel's reproof in Judges 2:2, "What is this you have done (NASB)?" The people did not comprehend just how broad and deep would be the effects of their disobedience though they had been warned many times. So, these nations, plus what was left of the original seven, became negative forces against Israel. More disobedience. The natural consequence was that they were no longer under God's protection. God allowed oppressors to subjugate Israel for a season. What the oppressors carried manifested in the nature of their cruelties to Israel. After a time, Israel would cry to God for mercy. In mercy God would then raise up a judge to deliver them. Peace and blessing reigned until the judge died. Then the cycle began again, worse than the previous time.

Prayer

Abba Father, You are holy. Your ways are higher than our ways and Your thoughts are higher than our thoughts. Your commands bring life and light to this darkened world.

You have commanded us, Your people, to be holy because You are. We confess we are not capable of this in our own strength. Philippians 2:13 tells us it is You, God, who works in us to will, to desire, and to act according to Your good purpose. So we come into Your presence with thanks and praise because Jesus, our Redeemer, has brought us into new life through faith in *His* obedience, *His* sacrifice, and *His* triumphant resurrection. We no longer want to conform to the ways of the world system; Holy Spirit, reveal them to us. Instead, we choose to put away from us the things that cloud our vision and compromise our thinking. We want to be yoked to Jesus and learn from Him.

In mercy show us errors in our thinking and understanding. Uncover the ungodly beliefs and lies we have been living under. Give us grace and humility to allow You to transform us. Fill us with Your Holy Spirit to enable us to follow after you with our whole heart, mind, and strength.

We pray all of this in the matchless name of Jesus Christ, Risen Savior, and Lord of all. Amen!

CHAPTER 3
The Aramean Curse
Weekly Readings

Day 1: Read Judges 3:6–11.

    Who is Othniel?
    Where have we met him previously? (Hint: see Judges 1)
    What does Othniel's history suggest to you?

Day 2: Read Judges 3:6-11 again.

    Who is Cushan Rishathaim? Google it!
    Think about Aram Naharaim, the nation that enslaved Israel. What can you find out about their history/culture?

Day 3: Read Matthew 9:6, 10:1, 28:18 and Luke 5:24.

What do these verses tell you about authority?

Day 4: Read Romans 13:1, Jude 25 and Revelation 2:26.

Who has ultimate authority, according to these scriptures?
How do you suppose authority and obedience are connected?

Day 5: Read John 14:15, 15:10 and 13:34. These speak of obedience, love, and commandments.

How are they related?

Day 6: Read John 2:1—11. This is the account of Jesus first public miracle in Cana, Galilee. We look at Jesus to see His strategy for dealing with problems.

Word Key

The following is a glossary of terms as applied to this study of Judges.

<u>Anointing</u>—the redemptive gifts, given to the Church, and assigned particularly to each believer by Holy Spirit, for the building up of the Body. There are seven spiritual gifts listed in Romans 12:6–8, which closely parallel the seven curses we look at in Judges.

<u>Cause</u>—chosen behaviors which bring about curse or blessing. For example, Deuteronomy 30:19 says, "This day I call heaven and earth as witnesses against you that I have set before you life and death, blessings and curses. Now choose life, so that you and your children may live and that you may love the LORD your God, listen to his voice, and hold fast to Him." The choice was to obey the commands of God or disobey.

<u>Generational Curse</u>—a pattern of demonic activity from generation to generation whereby the enemy of our souls arranges circumstances so that our energy, time, resources, etc. are devoured and our power to lay hold of our birthright is hindered.

<u>False Identity Statement/Legitimacy lie</u>—a fundamental belief, an ungodly belief in a lie concerning the root of one's value, legitimacy, and/or identity.

<u>Marker</u>—characteristic manifestations, signs, symptoms, or traits of a particular curse or blessing.

Othniel, the First Judge; Exploring Judges 3:6–11

Do you remember TV game shows? I was never a great fan, but I remember one show where the contestant was given a statement to which he had to answer with an appropriate question. With that idea in mind, what might be the right questions for this short passage in Judges 3? Who was Cushan Rishathaim? Where is Aram Naharaim? Who was Othniel? What does, "The Lord sold Israel into the hands of . . ." mean?

Look first at Judges 3:7. "The Israelites did evil in the eyes of the Lord." That should be no surprise in light of the introductory chapters of this book of Judges. Surprise or not, verse 8 describes the fierce anger of the Lord God with the phrase, *"sold* them into the hands of. . ." What does *sold* suggest? What other words might communicate the same idea?

When something, or in this case someone, is sold, it indicates a transfer of ownership. It becomes the property of the purchaser. In terms of a person, he/she is no longer free and independent. Rights, recourse to justice, property, self-government, etc. are forfeit. He is a slave, subject to his master. While slavery is illegal in western cultures, it still exists in our world. Slavery can be not only physical, but also emotional, mental, and spiritual, all with the same kinds of results. So, the scripture is saying that God sold Israel into slavery. Lest we begin to think that this was unfair of God, remember that God had warned Israel repeatedly (Exodus 34, Deuteronomy 7, Joshua 23, to cite a few examples), of the consequences for disobedience, rebellion, and apostasy. That was a clear teaching in the Old Covenant. What about now, now that Jesus has established the New Covenant in His blood? Jesus said, in Matthew 5:17, "Do not think that I came to abolish the Law or the Prophets, I did not come to abolish, but to fulfill (NASB)." John 8:31–59 records a discussion between Jesus and some Jews who were struggling to fully believe in Him. Verse 34: "Truly, truly I say to you, everyone who commits sin is the slave of sin (NASB)," this makes a pretty clear case that curses for sin continue. There are two great discourses on the theme of enslavement later in the New Testament: Romans 7 & 8 and Galatians 4 & 5. The point here is that whether New Testament or Old Testament, the problem is the need to deal with sin and its consequences. The children of Israel made a choice to sin grievously and the consequence here in Judges 3:8 was that they became slaves.

Israel was sold to Cushan-Rishathaim, king of western Mesopotamia. Who was this man and what can we know about him?

If you researched his name, you discovered that the name means "doubling of evil." Even with not much more than a name, we actually have a pretty good picture of this man, Cushan Rishathaim. "As we've seen in Scripture, a name is much more than nomenclature. It represents reputation and character. It reflects the heart of who someone is."[14] A man whom the Bible designates as "double evil" is very evil. The doubling aspect speaks of a generational dimension of his evil. His Father or Grandfather had been evil, perhaps sought power from evil sources in order to secure his dominion. That sin was then passed on, multiplying with the generations.

God had told His people to get rid of seven specific nations when they entered the Promised Land. Do you remember from Deuteronomy 18 some of the stated reasons?

One of the main offenses of the seven doomed nations was their pursuit of power and knowledge through all forms of witchcraft/sorcery. Then, as now, some people sought power and control over their own lives and things that concerned them. Others desired power/ruler-ship/dominion over much more than themselves and were willing to enter into vows and agreements with the powers of darkness in order to attain those goals. There were, and still are, immediate benefits to those vows. However, subsequent generations remained in bondage to the enemy with whom they had allied themselves. Evil grows, like weeds, wherever it can reach. One problem in resorting to evil was, and still is, that there is neither righteousness nor justice for the people. They were destined to live in bondage and fear. Talk about generational curses! Cushan-Rishathaim's father, or grandfather, most likely made alliances with wicked forces to gain power. Then, the dark anointing was passed in double portion, either actively—as in dedicating the son to the same dark master— or passively, as a generational curse from unrepentant sin.

Jeremiah 17:5 is one Scripture that declares God's perspective on our independence from Him. What does this verse say?

The pillars of God's throne are righteousness and justice. Mesopotamia is a land dominated by two rivers. Let's use them for an analogy. One river can represent the civil powers God has put in place to govern a nation. Remember that the apostle Paul wrote that we are to pray for kings and all leaders in authority because God instituted governments for our general welfare, (See Romans 13, Titus 3, and 1 Timothy 2). Let the other river represent the spiritual system, or Law, which is to govern the inner man and impact every area of life from the inside out. With the two rivers flowing freely, righteousness and justice were to abound, resources would flow to every area of life, and creativity would flourish.

In Israel God established Moses and Moses's council of elders for civil affairs and appointed Aaron, his sons, and the Levites to steward the spiritual life of the people. Together they led, trained, encouraged, and blessed the people. What happens when one "river" dominates both realms of governance?

Iran became a theocracy some years ago when their supreme spiritual leader also took over authority of the government. What had been a prosperous nation, beautiful in its product and honored in the world, became closed and hostile to all but a narrow group of like-minded people. Russia is a communist nation; political ideology has suppressed the spiritual. Fear, bondage, secrecy, dull greyness, and corruption plague her people. This is visible wherever the USSR was in power, despite years of liberation from its direct government. In God's Kingdom, the two rivers flow as the righteousness and justice which are the pillars of His throne. In Cushan-Rishathaim, we see a man who had come into alliance with evil spiritual forces, bringing the two rivers together in order to amass power and control—power with which he enslaved Israel.

After eight years of slavery, Israel finally came to her senses and cried out to the Lord. God raised up a man named Othniel. How much do we know about Othniel (Hint: look back at Judges 1:12–13)? What do you discover in this man that qualified him to serve as judge, or ruler, over Israel?

Did you notice that Othniel was related to a righteous and just man: his uncle, Caleb? Othniel acted in the same ways that Caleb had with regard to honoring God and man. That brought a generational blessing! Notice in Judges 3:9 that when God raised up Othniel to be Israel's deliverer, Othniel did not just take off and attack Cushan-Rishathaim. He waited for the empowering Spirit of the Lord, then he judged Israel. There was a period of cleansing and training.

1 Peter 4:12–5:11 and 2 Chronicles 7:13–14 both tell us that judgment begins in the household of God. We need to humble ourselves, seek God, and learn to see what God, in His righteousness, longs to show us so that we may be transformed. We need the righteous leaders Peter describes. These are things we can envision in Othniel. He led them in repentance. Then, when they went to war, the Lord gave Cushan-Rishathaim over into his hands. When we take the righteous inheritance that comes down our family line and build upon it the righteousness we receive by grace through faith in Jesus Christ, it gives God the room to take us to amazing places.

What were the results of Israel's repentance and forgiveness? Judges 3:10 tells us that Othniel went to war and the Lord delivered Israel from the cruel oppression of Cushan-Rishathaim. In Judges 3:11 we read that the land had forty years of rest. It is important to note that when we sin, it is not only people that are affected. Paul wrote in Romans 1 that all creation groans for the restoration of our Creator's order and design in the universe. In Nehemiah 9 we have a model for restoration. Nehemiah had called the nation together to repent for their sin and the sins of their fathers. This was a crucial step to be taken before the land and temple could be restored as God Himself had promised through the prophets. Until this realignment with God, the people continued to suffer under the weight of all that sin and judgment. Afterward, there was Divine favor to go forward in the restoration of the land, the temple, and the people. It was the same in Othniel's day as in Nehemiah's, and will be the same for us when we come into agreement with God and walk in obedience to Him.

Issues in the Aramean Curse

Let's think for a moment about the causes of Israel's subjugation to the Aramean Curse. (Aramean meaning from Aram, specifically Aram Naharaim.) Judges 3 says that Israel forgot their God and served Baal and Ashera. If you remember the Ten Commandments, those two items represent clear disobedience, compromise, and defiance of the God Who liberated the children of Israel. In addition, Israel had been instructed, through Moses and Joshua, to eradicate the seven nations in possession of the Promised Land, not to follow their ways or intermarry with them. Even if these sins crept up on the people of Israel, the fundamental issue seems to have been rebellion. In 1 Samuel 15:22–23 it says, "To obey is better than sacrifice, and to heed is better than the fat of rams. For rebellion is like the sin of divination, and arrogance like the evil of idolatry (NIV)." Israel was sold to a tyrant whose power was based in witchcraft, divination, and idolatry. The way back to favor with God was through recognition of their sin, repentance—turning to God alone—obedience, and true righteousness.

One other issue directly connected to Israel's rebellion was their relationship with authority. Moses had warned them before he died. Joshua had warned them before he died, too. Their rebellion was notorious: Deuteronomy 31:27 gives us a glimpse. What should have been their attitude to the laws of God and the leaders God appointed? What should be our attitude? Luke's Gospel relates an amazing story of Jesus that perfectly demonstrates a right understanding of authority. The centurion who made a request of Jesus in Luke 7:1–10 walked in a high level of civil authority. He recognized authority in Jesus, so when he asked Jesus to heal a valued servant, he also declined the honor of his own post (*i.e.*: ability to require subjects to come to him), in deference to Jesus's greater authority. He was a man with authority, and he knew how to live under authority. Matthew 16:24–26 gives us Jesus's instruction to His disciples concerning how we are to live under His authority and in the authority released, or delegated, in the Kingdom of God. Paul wrote in Romans 13:1–10 about the believers' relationship to earthly authorities. Hebrews 12:4–17 and 1 Peter 5 teach us about righteous perspectives as we face the challenges of life. Israel's rebellion against the authority of God in Judges 3 came under a curse of slavery and cruel oppression where justice, freedom, prosperity, and the favor of God were absent. When our issues match theirs, we can find ourselves under the Aramean curse.

Jesus's Alternative to the Aramean Curse

The Gospel of John records seven miracles of Jesus which demonstrate the righteous responses the Father desires of us. The first miracle in John 2:1–11 was also designated by John as the first public miracle of Jesus after His baptism. Let's look at what happened. Jesus, His disciples, His mother, and many others attended a wedding at Cana in Galilee. The passage tells us that when the wine was gone Mary went to Jesus and informed Him of the problem. Had Jesus been full of Himself instead of Holy Spirit, He could have replied something like, "No problem for Me, I can take care of that right away." However, without presumption or insult to Mary, He replied that essentially, it was not up to Him, but the Father, to determine the course of His actions. Mary must have been confident that the Father was interested in this problem because she instructed the servants to do whatever Jesus might tell them to do. We see here that Jesus had power and authority; Mary knew it and Jesus knew it. But, that authority was under the authority of the Father. Jesus had nothing to prove in fixing the problem of the wine. He was not eager to trumpet Himself as the 'fixer,' despite His obvious ability. At the right time, He gave instructions to the servants, whose obedience then brought about the miraculous provision of extraordinary wine. John's conclusion to this account states that this miracle revealed Jesus's glory and caused the disciples to put their faith in Him (John 2:11).

Earlier in John 1 we see the account of Jesus's baptism in the Jordan River. John the Baptist confirmed Jesus's anointing when he witnessed the Holy Spirit descending upon Jesus like a dove, and remaining on Him. The Holy Spirit empowered Jesus in the face of Satan's temptations. The same Holy Spirit enabled Jesus to operate fully in prophetic anointing. Here, in John 2, Mary made Jesus aware of the lack of wine, but Jesus discerned by the Spirit the *Father's* heart for the situation, the way that the problem should be remedied, the timing, and the desired outcome, which was far more than a sufficiency of wine. The gift of prophecy is meant to bring revelation, or insight, from Heaven concerning people, places, or things in the earth realm. From that revelation God releases His word of power to address the issue and activate resolution. Jesus waited upon God for revelation, timing, and instruction. Life flowed through that "prophetic" miracle in profound ways.

In the Luke 23 account of the crucifixion we read that Jesus's first words from the cross were "Father, forgive them for they know not what they do (NASB)." On the cross Jesus was "fixing" the sin problem for the whole world (John 3:16). None of the beneficiaries of this work had asked Jesus to do this. It was done without His receiving validation or appreciation, yet it brought about the most glorious redemption. Glory to God!

In conclusion, when you fix what God has given you to fix, using His supernatural power and resources, in His time, you have authority over the Aramean curse. God chose Othniel. Othniel used God's power to fix Israel's problem with Aram Naharaim. God sent Jesus to fix the sin problem (see Phil. 2). Jesus gave Himself fully to the task, using God's power, God's way, and in the end, achieved God's victory. Jesus said, "I have come that you might have life . . . (John 10:10, NIV)." The Apostle Paul wrote that, "God was in Christ reconciling the world to Himself. . .(2 Cor. 5:19, NIV). " And in 1 John 3:8 (NIV), we read that "Jesus came to destroy the works of the devil." **This is our model as well as our Messiah.**

Application Points

1. The <u>cause </u>for God's judgment was Israel's rebellion and sin.
2. The <u>generational sin</u> that manifested in the Aramean curse was that someone sought lawless power or solutions in wrong ways, (witchcraft and occult arts, rebellion)
3. The identifying <u>markers </u>of the Aramean curse are that:
   a. One cannot solve problems with natural/civil law (No justice)
   b. Earned resources never get to you (No wages for slaves)
   c. In any conflict, circumstances never fall in your favor.
4. The <u>redemptive gift</u> that parallels this curse is the gift of prophecy: specifically, the ability to see clearly and to speak in such a way as to activate God's solutions. Perspective, organization of information, solutions, and ability to foresee consequences/outcomes are inherent to this gift. The prophet releases revelation that can bring about resolution.
5. The <u>false identity statement </u>that corrupts this gift and is prone to manifest in this curse is, "I am ok when I can use my abilities and natural law to fix problems." Jesus perfectly models the heart attitude and mindset for the prophet. Submit everything to God. Fix what God directs according to His ways and His timing, for His glory alone.
6. The <u>blessing </u>when the Aramean curse is broke is that one is able to establish and access a proper legal system and justice both civilly and spiritually.

Prayer of Renunciation and Cleansing

Father God, I thank You and praise You that I can come boldly to Your throne of grace because of Jesus. Thank You for sending Your Son to be my Passover Lamb. I am Your child because of the redemption He bought for me with the shedding of His blood. I praise and honor You for the grace that His sacrifice applies to every sin. I am covered by Christ's blood and live in a new covenant relationship.

The scripture tells me that it is for freedom that Jesus sets us free; we are not to remain in bondage. For this reason I come with a petition. This New Covenant gives me specific legal rights: I have the right to be free from the enemy's control. I have a right to possess my God-given birthright. I have a right to reap good things where I have sown good seed. I ask that You open the books in every branch of my family lines. In them, identify every individual who has come under the Aramean curse. I ask You to identify every legitimacy lie that was believed—every person that solved a problem that was not theirs to solve, and every person who failed to solve a problem that was their assignment. I ask You to identify any individual who chose to use occult power to solve problems. I hereby stand in the gap for these sins of my family line and renounce them as rebellion against Your authority, Your ways, and Your timing. I ask that all these incidents be covered with the blood of the Lord Jesus Christ. I also repent for any ways I have allowed myself to be shaped by the sins of past generations, for any ways I have believed the lie that my legitimacy comes from solving problems, and for any way I have participated in those same behaviors. I reject and renounce these as sin and ask for Your forgiveness and cleansing.

You are the Holy God. The pillars of Your throne are justice and righteousness. I acknowledge that it was just for this curse to come into my family line because there are wages for sin as well as righteousness. I acknowledge Your justice in allowing the enemy to devour in my family line because of these rebellious choices. You are the God of mercy and love. I believe this because You sent Jesus to be our Redeemer. His shed blood has the power to break this curse. So now, because of my renunciation and Your promise in 1 John 1:9, that when we repent You are faithful and just to forgive us our sin, I receive the cleansing of His blood. By the delegated authority in Jesus Christ my Lord, I say to this curse that you have no place anymore in me or my family. Furthermore, in the Name of Jesus Christ, I command every devouring spirit connected with this curse and every facet of this curse to leave me, my family, and my physical and spiritual seed, and never return. I ask You, Father, to build in me a fortress of righteousness, justice, and love where this place of darkness existed. Pour out Your Spirit on me. Teach me how to walk in and under authority. As I yield myself as a living sacrifice, show me how to make right choices in relationship with authority. Holy Spirit, help me to teach my physical and spiritual seed Your ways.

Now I call back the blessings and favor that have been stolen. I call forth the birthright and inheritance that have been intended for me and my physical and spiritual seed. I thank You in advance for Your grace and mercy as You work in my life, completing the work You have begun. Lord, be glorified. I pray this in the Name of Jesus Christ my Lord. Amen and amen!

CHAPTER 4
The Moabite Curse
Weekly Readings

Day 1: Read Genesis 13, focusing on verses 9 and 10.

In this account we find Abram and Lot resolving an issue.
What does this process tell you about the characters of these two men?

Day 2: Read Genesis 19.

How does character show up in the choices made by each person?

How, then, do the choices impact outcomes?

In spite of the character question, how do you think God sees Lot?

Why?

Day 3: Read Judges 3:12—31.

Put on your detective hat and search for clues.

What is unusual in this account?

What is stated, or omitted, that brings up questions for you?

Day 4: Read John 4:40—54 and Luke 23:34.

What do you see in the mood of the crowd around Jesus?

How did Jesus respond to the invitation/command to serve the Royal Official's need?

Why that way?

Day 5: Read Deuteronomy 32:8, Psalm 74:17, Proverbs 8:29 and 15:25.

From these passages, what do you see about the significance of boundaries to God?

Day 6: Read John 15:1—11.

What do you see about boundaries in this text?

The Moabites: Genesis 13 & 19

Who were the Moabites? Where did they come from? What difference does all this make? Let's break it down.

In Genesis 13 we observe Abram and Lot making a strategic decision. They had prospered in this new land so that living together was creating tensions. Abram proposed a solution. What were the options? How was the problem finally resolved? More importantly, what can you discern about Lot's character in this scene?

Upon whom and what did Lot focus in making his choice? Abraham actually deferred to his younger nephew. Lot moved his household and flocks into the fertile plains to the East. Soon, he was in the city itself. The trouble was, God spoke to His friend Abraham some time later about the deep wickedness in Sodom and Gomorrah. He planned to destroy those cities. That put Lot at risk. In Genesis 18:16 and following, we can read Abraham's fervent intercession on behalf of Lot and the righteous citizens who were in judgment's way. Ultimately, God agreed with Abraham to spare the cities if there were ten righteous.

When trouble came, in Genesis 19, what did it mean for Lot and his family?

How would you feel if you were one of Lot's daughters?

What are the pros and cons of Lot's behavior, as you see him?

Why do you think his intended sons-in-law would not believe him?

What can we know about Lot's wife? Not much is said about her, but think about the possible reasons for her "looking back." Look for God's perspective. Write what you discover.

When Lot realized that the destruction forewarned by the angels was actually happening, he reacted in fear, retreating to the caves/mountains outside Zoar. Genesis 19:30—38 presents the tragic outcome of Lot's foolishness. How were his daughters affected by this drastic change of life?

What became of their plan to secure a future and a hope for themselves? Who instigated? Who followed along and why?

What were the results of their actions for Lot's family? For Israel?

If Lot had obeyed the Angel in the first place, how might the whole story be different?

Exploring the Story: Judges 3:12—31

Read this account of Israel's interaction with the Moabites. Now, finish the sentence: "Once again the Israelites. . . ."

Who is Eglon? Whom did King Eglon gather around him to assist in overtaking Israel? Is there anything significant about these allies?

Eglon's strategy included defeating Israel by taking possession of the City of Palms. What is significant about that city?

How long did Israel serve Eglon, King of Moab? When Israel cried out to the LORD, in verse 15, the LORD raised up a judge, or deliverer for them. Who is this deliverer and what is unique about him?

The tribute plays a key role in Israel's emancipation from Moab. By definition, a tribute is "a stated sum or other valuable consideration paid by one sovereign or state to another in acknowledgment of subjugation or as the price of peace."[15] Obligation and enforced taxation are indicated. The word in Scripture used for the tribute Ehud brought to King Eglon is *minchah*, indicating a gift-type tribute. This suggests a gift given to appease, a bribe. Later, in the reigns of King David and King Solomon, tributes were required of conquered peoples, but these tributes were explicitly defined assessments of gold, goods, produce, etc, like taxes. What kinds of issues might Eglon's annual *minchah* present for Israel?

It is also interesting to think about the fact that Israel, being a theocracy, had no human sovereign. Ehud, whom God chose to judge, was in a unique position.

Now, think about the strategy Ehud devised to bring about Israel's deliverance from Moabite oppression. What was the plan?

Why do you think Ehud sent away the rest of the team who delivered the tribute instead of using all of them to take down the King? Do you think this was this something of a suicide mission?

The next phase of Ehud's strategy was to rally the troops and retake the ford of the Jordan and the City of Palms. In what ways does this become significant for Israel?

Much later, the prophet Jeremiah spoke of God's judgment on Moab. Jeremiah 48 is an enlightening read after this account in Judges.

Looking to Jesus

Up to this point in this study, we have focused on the Moabites—their origin in Lot's family and the generational perpetuation of self-serving indulgence and neglect concerning obligations and boundaries. In contrast, we discovered that God raised up Ehud, an unselfish, righteous strategist who risked his own life to begin the emancipation of Israel by executing Eglon, the Moabite king. Immediately after that, Ehud and his army pursued the re-establishment of Israel's borders and sovereignty over the Promised Land. There is in Ehud a sample of the type of hands-on service, or ministry, which Romans 12 calls the redemptive gift of service.

Jesus Christ is not only the Messiah-Redeemer, but also our model in all aspects of life, spiritual and otherwise. In Paul's letter to the Christ-followers in Philippi, we read a beautiful description of Jesus's servant heart.

READ Philippians 2:6—11. What do you see there concerning:

- Jesus's origin
- Jesus's primary, or first, attitude
- Jesus's role as a man
- Extent of Jesus's service
- The outcome

Now turn to John 4:40—54. There we see Jesus in the midst of ministry opportunities. What we do not see is any way Jesus maneuvered to call attention to Himself or advance Himself in the eyes of the people. What is the record of verses 40—42 highlighting as the end result of Jesus's conversation with the woman at the well?

Moving into verses 43—45, what seems to be the prevailing attitude in Galilee toward Jesus?

From verse 46 on: What are the implications of a "royal official" coming to Jesus and begging Him to travel the approximately twenty miles to Capernaum in order to heal his son? What issues and expectations were possibly at work?

Jesus gave the official a choice: believe and go without Jesus, or stay and try to manipulate Jesus into compliance. Do you think there was a greater purpose in the manner of Jesus's interaction with the royal official? What might it have been?

Ultimately, what was the outcome for the official and his son?

We can see here that Jesus was not pressed into conformity to the peoples' demands, or even needs, in order to prove Himself. The signs and wonders were the evidence of who He was and they flowed from the FATHER's plan and purpose. Though He was viewed without honor in Galilee, Jesus acted *honorably and consistently with His birthright and the destiny He came to fulfill.* Even on the cross (see Luke 23:43), though naked and deprived of justice and mercy, in His full Kingliness, Jesus said to the believing thief, "Today you shall be with Me in paradise." He operated in His authority to declare this transaction, but He stayed on the cross until the assigned task was finished.

Now, review Ehud's service to God and Israel in light of Jesus's own example.

Think what this model of service, or ministry, should look like in us, for our day.

Application Points

1. The <u>cause</u> for this curse was Israel's sin.
2. The <u>generational sin</u> that manifested in this curse is that you or someone in your family line, took freedom in the wrong way when freedom had not been granted, or chose to be passive under bondage.
3. The <u>markers of the Moabite curse</u> center around boundary issues. Personal boundaries are regularly violated, particularly in relationships. Resources are devoured before they reach you. Those in authority over you fail to build a platform for you to achieve your birthright.
4. The <u>parallel anointing</u> from Romans 12 is the servant anointing. Characteristically, the servant sees physical needs of others and moves to meet them so that need is no longer a hindrance. Life can flow. People are helped.
5. The <u>legitimacy lie</u> that corrupts the servant anointing is that "In order to feel legitimate I must meet your need, make it possible for you to succeed, or build a platform for your success." This is accompanied by an inability to say no or set personal limits. Often, we recognize this in its extreme as enabling, or co-dependency. At the very least, it is service with a personal agenda.
6. The <u>blessing</u> when this curse is broken is that one is able to establish healthy, secure boundaries, with freedom to expand as God ordained, from a foundation or platform that He supernaturally provides.

Prayer of Renunciation and Cleansing

FATHER GOD, I come into Your presence with thanksgiving and praise to You, Jehovah-Jireh, the Lord who provides. You have provided the family as a vehicle of birthright and inheritance. You have provided seasons in our lives: seasons of childhood and adulthood, of learning and growing, of teaching and equipping, and seasons of being nurtured and being the nurturer. You bestow authority in parents and others for seasons of following and of leading. I understand and proclaim that with these provisions come responsibilities. I acknowledge that the proper order of life is for those in authority to build a platform for those under their authority to lay hold of their birthright, then to release them at the proper time. Thank You for Your good provision.

FATHER, I ask that You open the books in my family lines. I ask You to identify every event where there was an authority, either in my lines or over my lines, who failed to build up and release those entrusted to them. I proclaim this was contrary to Your design and so renounce it as sin. I ask You to expose every situation where someone chose to embrace family peace at the expense of possessing their birthright. I declare that is sin, and reject and renounce those sins. I ask You to identify every incident where someone took their freedom wrongly in order to gain their birthright, and declare that is sin. I reject and renounce those events. In the Name of Jesus, I ask You to cover these generational sins with Christ's atoning blood. Furthermore, every way that my own behaviors and attitudes have repeated those generational sins, I now reject, renounce, and ask for Your forgiveness and cleansing.

I acknowledge that it was just and right for the Moabite curse to be in my family line because we violated Your covenantal Law. But, I rejoice that You provided the Lamb of God to be my atonement. By faith I stand. By His blood I am made holy. By His blood I am made clean. Glory to Jesus!

Now, in the delegated authority of Jesus Christ, I command every devouring spirit that used to be empowered by the Moabite curse to leave me, my spouse, and my physical and spiritual seed and never return. FATHER, You are the righteous Judge of all. As these events have been washed by Jesus's blood, I ask You to enforce these righteous decrees. I ask You, FATHER, to enlarge my boundaries and to give me freedom of movement and resources to accomplish everything You have desired me to accomplish. I declare Ephesians 2:8—10, "For by grace you have been saved through faith; and that not of yourselves, it is the gift of God; not of works, that no one should boast. For we are His workmanship, created in Christ

Jesus for good works, which God prepared beforehand that we should walk in them." I ask You to fill all the places where this curse and its effects have now been removed with Your Holy Spirit. Teach me how to walk in Your ways. Let the works for which I was created, be done, to the glory of Father, Son, and Holy Spirit. I ask now, in accordance to Your Word, that You release the generational blessing of peace and secure borders to me, my spouse, and my physical and spiritual seed.

I thank You by faith in advance, in the Name of the Lord Jesus Christ, Who alone is worthy of all praise, honor, glory, and power, forever and ever. Amen and Amen!

CHAPTER 5
The Canaanite Curse
Weekly Readings

Day 1: Read Judges, chapters 4 & 5. Briefly summarize this unique account.

    Jot down any insights/revelations/questions that arose from that reading.

Day 2: Read Genesis 9 (focus on verses 20–27).

    This is where we are introduced to Canaan.
    Who was he?
    What happened?

Day 3: Read Genesis 10:6 and 12:5—7.

    What more do you learn about Canaan?

Does this stir any memories from previous Bible study?

Day 4: Read the following passages: Romans 12:8, Acts 20:1—3 & Luke 3:16—18.

What do you learn about exhortation from these Scriptures?

Day 5: More references about exhortation: Hebrews 3:13; 12:19—25 & 13:20—22.

Is exhortation important?
Why or why not?

Day 6: Read John 6:1—15.

As you read this miracle account, think about how Jesus operated in the gift of exhortation.

Who Were the Canaanites?

Genesis 9, 10:6 & 15–19, 12:5–7

*****Before we look at the Canaanites we need to think about the small, but significant, details in Judges 3:31. Why is this strange event recorded here with no explanation and no resolution?*****

From the passage in Genesis 9, we read that the world-wide flood has subsided. Noah's family has moved out of the ark, and established a home and a vineyard. Life was good! But already trouble came to the new paradise. What happened (verses 22—23)?

Apparently, Noah was more than a little perturbed over what he learned when he arose out of his drunken stupor. Why does the text say, "Ham, the father of Canaan, saw the nakedness of his father."?

Think critically. Genesis 10:6 shows us that Canaan was the fourth son of Ham. What kind of clues does that suggest?

Genesis 9:24 says, "When Noah awoke from his wine he knew what his youngest son had done." What could this possibly mean?

Noah cursed his grandson Canaan. Now, think about the results of living under a curse. As someone pointed out, we are all under a curse because of what Adam and Eve did, but we each still have free will. The choices we make each day have consequences. Look at Canaan. What became of his family? If you look at Genesis 10:15—19 you will see that four of the descendants of Canaan are among the seven nations God instructed Israel to annihilate (Deuteronomy 7). Deuteronomy 18:10—13 describes where these nations had sunk to in their depravity. The reproofs of life did not turn them from their sin. They lost the opportunity for blessing and became degenerate cultures and cruel oppressors. It is just as God instructed Israel through Moses: obedience = blessing; disobedience = curses. The good news for us is that, in Christ, curses can be broken.

A Story With-in a Story

Judges 4 & 5

If you only read chapter 4 you will certainly have a general understanding of what transpired in Israel following Ehud and Shamgar. For the fuller picture you must read chapter 5—a story within the story. There are many clues in Deborah's song as to what was going on in chapter 4. Notice in Judges 4:1—3 that God again "sold" Israel into the hands of a foreign power. Who were the principle characters oppressing Israel? How did they oppress Israel? For how long?

What would it be like to live under a curse for twenty long years? What kind of mindset takes over in such a circumstance? A couple of more current examples may help us understand. In Iraq, during the early 21st century, many wondered why the people of Iraq did not rise up against the tyrant, Saddam Hussein, even after Coalition forces removed him from power. There was a reluctance to act on their own behalf. One thing was obvious: fear reigned. They feared retribution from any number of possible sources. Deeper than fear, perhaps, was a belief system that had saturated these oppressed people—one of powerless-ness, passivity, don't-rock-the-boat, I am just one person, who can you trust anyway?

We witnessed another example of this bondage when we had the opportunity to travel to Kyrgyzstan in 2009 to welcome the birth of our eleventh grandchild. That country had been part of the former USSR. Though it was a beautiful country, rich in natural resources and potential, darkness pervaded the capitol city. The most profound realization we came to was that corruption had become a way of life for most everyone—a means of survival.

As we step into Judges 4, we see Israel in a similar frame of mind to our contemporary examples. We also recognize very quickly that the way God dealt with the Canaanites is much different under Deborah's leadership than the previous judges' tactics. How did she set up the deliverance of her people, under God's directives? Who was Barak and what was his assignment? Why do you think he balked at Deborah's exhortation? What were the consequences for Barak before any battle even began?

Who were the Kenites? What have they to do with Israel and Canaan?

How did the enemy general end up in Jael's tent with a tent-peg through his head?

From the clues in our account of Deborah and Barak, let's piece together what living must have been like in Israel. First, we see that in Judges 4:3 they were severely oppressed for 20 years. In 5:6—8 we get the clue that the people did not dare travel on the highways, but took round about paths instead. The valleys where the richest, most productive land was were controlled by the Canaanites, leaving Israel to scratch out an existence. They also had no weapons—nothing for self-defense, much less for mounting an army. In Judges 5:8—12, it sounds like it was the peasantry who finally took action. Where were the leaders? Where were the men?

What was God's strategy for subduing the 900 iron chariots that ruled the fertile plains? See Judges 5. How could they face an enemy armed with nine hundred chariots and unknown quantities of weapons? Well, the glory was that God fought for them. The rains came, the river rose, and the chariot wheels sank in mud to the point that the Canaanites had to abandon them. Wow! Israelite forces were able to take the advantage and use the enemy's own weapons against them.

The descriptions of a fearful Barak, female leadership, and village life in light of the terrorizing by iron charioteers, paint a pretty grim picture. Think about what had happened to their society. What issues do you see in Judges 5:9—18?

Can you recognize any similar issues in our day, either broadly in the culture or in your personal experiences?

Verses 24—30 present two more scenes. What do they mean? Finally, in verse 31, we read a beautiful benediction. What is the blessing for Israel?

Exhortation, the Parallel Redemptive Gift

As we have looked at Israel under the cruel and exploitive domination of the Canaanites, we have good cause to ask where all the men have gone. How extraordinary that such a strong patriarchal society should be willing to turn to a woman for leadership! Now, in the 21rst century after Jesus, we have difficulty not relegating this to sexism. But it is significant on many levels, not the least of which being that God is not sexist. He is willing to use whoever is available, willing to seek the LORD, and to walk in obedience. Deborah fit the requirements, so God established Deborah as judge in Israel. From the record in Judges 4 and 5 we see that Deborah functioned in wisdom as judge, prophet, and exhorter.

The redemptive gift, from Romans 12, parallel to the Canaanite curse, is the gift of exhortation. Webster defines exhortation as "an utterance, discourse, or address conveying urgent advice or recommendation."[16] The Bible's definition adds to Webster's the aspect of coming alongside, encouraging, consoling, and comforting. Biblical exhortation, then, is an appeal to walk in certain ways for the strengthening and establishing of a believer's faith and confidence in God, as well as an appeal to specific actions in obedience to God. There is a "natural" aspect to this gift that we recognize as an exceptional ability to communicate. For the believer operating in this spiritual gift of exhortation there is to be a draw on the supernatural resources of Heaven that gives power to the word of exhortation, which activates a response in the hearts and minds of the hearers. Thus, an exhorter speaks with power and authority.

The first thing we see in Deborah as judge, is a recognition of her authority. People came to her for wise counsel and judgments. The second thing we see, in her interaction with Barak, is the power of her God-inspired words to bring Barak and the nation to action. Though he refused to go to battle unless Deborah accompanied him, Barak did summon the volunteer army and move out under the instruction Deborah gave. All that Deborah foretold came about. In Judges 5, the song of Deborah and Barak is also an exhortation in that it not only clearly recalls the battle, but sets forth the many reasons Israel should trust and worship Jehovah alone.

Much of the prophetic and apostolic literature in both old and new testaments of the Bible is exhortation in nature. Certainly, the *Shema* in Deuteronomy, "Hear, o Israel, the Lord our God is one. You shall love the Lord your God with all your heart, with your entire mind and with all your strength," is an exhortation. In Galatians 5:1, the apostle Paul exhorts the believers that, "It is for freedom that Christ has set us free. Stand firm therefore and do not be subject again to a yoke of slavery." There are many other exhortations for us throughout the Scriptures. 1 Corinthians 3:4—9; 4:1—2, 2 Timothy 3:2, and Romans 12:4 contain instructions about the gift of exhortation. In every case the gifts God gives through the Holy Spirit are for the purpose of building up and maturing the Body of Christ. This demonstrates a positive life-flow; from God's resources to those in need. Therefore, we 21st century believers can still experience the gift of exhortation today—speaking the mind and heart of God, with the power of God, for the glory of God, and the building up of the Body.

What Would Jesus Do?

Let's look again at our example, Jesus, in the fourth miracle in John's Gospel: John 6:1—15. The opening statement in this chapter tells us that Jesus left the intensity of the aftermath of the healing at the pool of Bethesda for the peace of the Sea of Galilee. There is no doubt that the retreat was to serve both Jesus and the disciples. Remember that Jesus was fully aware of the time—the season of His ministry before the cross. He knew the absolute necessity of preparing the twelve disciples to take this Gospel of the Kingdom into the whole world. The clamoring and demands of the crowd regularly imposed on the time needed to sow into His disciples. However, Jesus never lost sight of His mission regarding the multitudes or the disciples. In this account, Jesus uses the great multitude who had followed them to teach the disciples several very important lessons. Verse six actually says Jesus tested them! One small boy came with a lunch. God used it to feed a multitude of 5000. After all had eaten and were satisfied Jesus instructed the disciples to do what?

Think about all that had just happened. Can you summarize, in your own words, at least one lesson to be gained in this amazing miracle from the perspective of a disciple? There are many.

The crowds were curious, sated, amazed, and then determined. Verse 14 sums up their conclusion. What was that?

Jesus had a different idea. What does John 6:15 tell us?

Later, in another encounter with the crowd, presumably some of the same ones who had been fed on the mountainside, Jesus declared, "Truly I say to you, you seek Me not because you saw signs, but because you ate of the loaves and were filled. Do not work for the food which perishes, but for the food which endures to eternal life which the Son of Man shall give to you, for on Him the FATHER, even GOD, has set His seal (John 6:26, NIV)." Throughout the whole of these events we see Jesus leading—leading and exhorting the disciples about the priorities of the Kingdom, the resources of the Kingdom, the timing of the FATHER, and the eternal nature that is to be our perspective. He ministered mightily and intentionally to the great multitude by providing for their physical needs—food and healing—and their spiritual needs in the instructions before, during, and after the miracle itself. His leadership never served Himself. He was not driven by the needs of the crowd or of the disciples, but by the commission of the FATHER.

Jesus built no organization that needed to be sustained. Life flowed principally from Jesus to the disciples. Jesus never held back from speaking the truth for fear of losing followers. His legitimacy rested in intimacy with God the Father and perfect obedience to His will.

When the crowd of 5000 whom He had fed pressed Him to be their King, Jesus withdrew alone to a quiet place to pray. This is the opposite of exploitive leadership and the Canaanite curse.

On the cross Jesus made no outcry against His persecutors, or the executioners, or the deserters among His followers. Jesus surrendered to the full cost of obedience to the purpose of His Father. There was no denial or entitlement. He took full ownership of the work God had sent Him to do. His heart was broken when He cried out, "My God, my God, why have YOU forsaken Me?"

Application Points

1. The <u>cause</u> for God's judgment was Israel's sin.
2. The <u>generational sin</u>: The root cause of this curse is exploitation from within. Someone used their influence to induce follower(s) to do wrong, often in the area of moral impurity. Other contributing causes include needing people to need what one has to offer; holding people back instead of releasing them; an inability to confront sin because the leader needs their favor. A question to be asked with this curse: am I under exploitive leadership or being an exploitive leader?
3. <u>Markers:</u> The principle marker of the Canaanite curse is living under an exploitive abusive leader or relationship as if under an iron fist. Often a person under this curse seems to go from one abusive leader to another. The Canaanites cruelly oppressed Israel with iron chariots, took the resources of the fertile river valleys leaving people to scrabble and scrounge for survival. This kind of leader sucks the life out of the followers. He or she is uninterested in, or unable to, equip and release the people into their birthrights. This sort of leader typically makes promises he cannot keep and places demands on people which they must sacrifice to fulfill. Because life flows from the followers to the leader, the consequences of poor leadership and the reproofs of life are often denied. (A good, positive leader may also make large demands of his people, but not without including himself in the demand, and always with appreciation and affirmation for the efforts of his followers. He is likely to promote

and advance followers who serve well and is careful to fulfill promises. Life flows from leader to followers.)

Another strong marker of the Canaanite curse is that time is devoured so that it is impossible for one to develop one's own resources. Consequently, the one under this curse is never able to step into his/her birthright.

4. <u>Parallel redemptive gift</u>: the gift of exhortation

5. <u>Legitimacy lie</u>: I am legitimate when I have followers—people around me who depend upon or are subject to my leadership. While the gift of exhortation intuitively operates in a charismatic type of leadership, this lie presupposes a need to have followers. Therefore, the exhorter living in agreement with this lie must work to get and keep followers, often by any means. They tend to deny the negative results of their manipulations or feel entitled to positive outcomes despite the real cause and effect sequence.

6. <u>Blessing</u> when this curse is broken: one is released to fully develop the God-given birthright, with time, money, and mentorship resources. Like Moses, we are able to lead slaves to son-ship. Intimacy and obedience are keys to walking in to this blessing in fullness.

Prayer of Renunciation and Cleansing

Almighty God and Father, I proclaim that You are the source of life and You are the source of authority. You possess absolute authority, yet it is the most life-giving authority that the universe has ever known. I worship You because You are good and always good. As Your child through faith, I live under Your authority, yet I acknowledge that my forefathers as well as I, myself, have failed to walk faithfully in and under this life-giving authority. I ask You to open the books of my family lines and shine Your light on every event that invited the Canaanite curse.

I reject and renounce the following:

- The belief that legitimacy can be established through popularity;
- The sin of using popularity to normalize iniquity, especially in the areas of moral purity;
- Shifting consequences for my bad choices to those under me;
- The perversion of invoking love, loyalty, or submission in order to force someone under me to pay the price for my sin;

- The deception of behaving in supposed love, loyalty, or submission by paying the price of someone else's sin;
- The spirit of entitlement which compromises proper stewardship of God-given vision;
- And, the sin of staying in an abusive situation in order to maintain peace and comfort at the expense of possessing my birthright.

I agree that these are sin. Wherever they are present in my life and my family line I ask for forgiveness and cleansing as You have promised in 1 John 1:9. In mercy, let the Blood of Jesus cover every vestige of the Canaanite curse. I now receive that cleansing.

In the Name of Jesus Christ, by the authority delegated to me as a child of God, I now renounce every demonic structure and entity that was empowered by these sins and iniquities, and I command them to leave me and my family and to never return. In every place where this curse had taken root, I ask You, Holy Spirit, to fill me with Your truth, vision, and life. As I yield myself afresh to be a living sacrifice, renew my mind with the mind of Christ. Grant me Your strategies and timing to eradicate all the Canaanite influences in my life. Teach me what is Your "normal," so I won't fall back into old patterns. Draw me into a place where I have the time and permission to nurture the gifts that You have given me. In Your great mercy and grace, release the blessings that have been robbed or held back because of this Canaanite curse to me, my spouse, and my physical and spiritual seed.

I love You, Lord God. I bless You and thank you through Jesus Christ, my Redeemer. Amen.

CHAPTER 6
The Midianite Curse
Weekly Readings

Day 1: Read the beginning of the Midianites in Genesis 25:1—11.

    In your own words, summarize how the Midianites came to be.

    What is your initial response to this account?

Day 2: Now read Judges 6:1—8:32.

    This is the longest passage in the Judges thus far.

    What strikes you as significant in this episode?

Day 3: Reading more about the Midianites and their interaction with Israel, look at Numbers 22:1—7, 23:18—26 and 24:1—2 and 10.

In each passage, what do you see about Midian and Israel?

Day 4: Numbers 25:6—18 records another costly affair between Midianites and Israelites. Read Numbers 31:1—3 contains God's instructions concerning Midian.

What lessons do you glean from these passages?

What questions do you glean from these passages?

Day 5: Read all of John 9.

Think about Jesus's words and actions in contrast to Abraham's and Midian's.

Day 6: The following scriptures are among many that speak about <u>giving</u>. John 3:16, Matthew 10:8, 42; 11:28; 19:21 and 20:28.

What do you learn about giving from God's perspective?

Who Were the Midianites?

Let's start in Genesis 25:1—11 to discover who these people were and where they came from? Read the passage as many times as necessary to recognize what kind of dynamics were "at play" here.

The six sons born to Abraham after Sarah had died were all given gifts and sent away to the east. One of those sons was Midian. How would you feel about your father if this had happened to you?

How would you feel about the older half-brother who received all the inheritance?

This was not an inconsequential choice on Abraham's part, was it? Do you feel what Abraham did was right or best? Why or why not?

The next time we see the Midianites is in Exodus 2. The Israelites had become slaves in exile in Egypt. Moses, set apart by God for a unique task, had grown up in Pharaoh's court, groomed as a prince of Egypt. As a young adult his interactions with both the Hebrew slaves and an Egyptian slave master landed him in trouble, so he fled for his life to Midian. There, he was given grace by a priest of Midian and his family. While living in Midian God taught Moses the skills of a shepherd in preparation for his destiny. Eventually, Moses's father in law joined the Israelites in the Promised Land (Exodus 18:1—27).

The Midianites appear again in Numbers 22—25 and 31. The long passage in Numbers 22-24 tells the story of Balak, king of Moab, who enlisted the kings of Midian to help deal with Israel. Specifically, they hired Balaam, a seer, to come curse Israel using his powers of divination. If you do not know this story you should read through it. Even though Balaam was practicing occult arts, God spoke to him. He was told to go with the messengers of King Balak, but to only say what God would tell him. Balaam ended up blessing Israel in all three attempts to curse them. The first two "tries," Balaam relied on his witchcraft. But, the third time the Scripture tells us he did not resort to his arts. Instead, he faced the plain where the Israelites were encamped and listened. Then, he spoke and declared that his eyes had been opened. Again, blessing came forth instead of the required curse. Wouldn't you think that Balaam would have realized that God is the only God? The next thing we know, we discover that Balaam, unable to earn the king's reward by cursing, had suggested instead a devious scheme to corrupt Israel by sending Moabite women into their camp to seduce the Israelites. Scriptures tell us how God dealt with Balaam's and Midian's treachery.

At this point, it seems beneficial to return to Deuteronomy 18:9—15 to review the things God had declared detestable. These served as grounds for the instructions to Israel to remove the seven occupying nations.

Obviously, there are consequences for the choices we make—the seeds we sow. Check out the following scriptures:

- Psalm 126:5—6
- Proverbs 22:7—9
- Luke 6:38
- Galatians 6:6—10

When you have been slighted or abused in some way, what do you do about it? The Bible tells us to deal right away with our anger or we will give the devil a foothold. If we continue in a pattern of thought, belief, or action which is contrary to God's way it can become a stronghold. Is it possible that we are seeing this in the Midianites? What about in your own life?

Midianites in the Book of Judges

It seems that Moses and the Israelite army did not annihilate *all* of the Midianites in Numbers 31 for here they are in Judges 6—8. Look at the first ten verses of Judges 6. Curious, is it not, who Midian enlisted to help them against Israel?

What was the Midianite strategy against Israel?

This seems to be a clear example of taking vengeance versus giving grace. The Israelites were brought very low, causing them to cry out to the Lord. What was God's response to their appeal?

Did God totally abandon Israel? In Judges 6:11—24 we read of a visitation by the Angel of the Lord. What would you do if you were visited by an angel? Would you even know it was an angel? Did Gideon? Look at the conversation and describe what was taking place.

Now compare Gideon's reactions with Barak's from the Canaanite oppression.

Another interesting comparison is between this account and each of the first three in the book of Judges. In the Aramean and Moabite records it says that God raised up a deliverer. With the Canaanite oppression scripture says there was a prophetess who was judging Israel at the time; God used her. Now we see an angel sent to give an assignment to Gideon. What was the word from the angel?

God often required an act of obedience to follow a prophetic revelation. In Judges 6:25—27 we read what was demanded of Gideon. What was it?

Why, do you suppose, did Gideon do it at night?

What reaction did Gideon's obedience garner from the townsfolk?

From his own father?

What is the significance of Joash changing Gideon's name to Jerubaal? Remember the power and purpose of names.

Here is a possible explanation for the confusing response of father, Joash, to son, Gideon. Joash wanted to protect his son from the murderous intent of the townspeople. At the same time, he was probably angry over what was done. They were his bulls and his altars to the foreign gods, after all! The incensed mob was rebuffed, even threatened with reprisals should they act against Gideon. But Joash renamed his son Jerubaal, which means "let Baal contend against him," effectively giving that pagan entity permission to vindicate itself.

On the heels of the outcry of the town against Gideon, enemy forces from Midian, allied with the Amalekites, crossed into Israel and encamped in preparation for war. The end of

Judges 6 and into Judges 7 details events that helped Gideon step into the leadership that the Angel had announced: confirmation with the fleeces, calling together the volunteer army, the refining of that mass of volunteers down to 300, and God's stated purpose. Why do you suppose God directed Gideon as He did?

What did the Lord say about sending all but 300 warriors home?

One of the hardest things for us is understanding the difference between acting in our own strength and just being obedient so that God can work through us. Do you struggle with this? Why do you think Gideon needed the confirming signs?

What do the signs show us about God?

Judges 7:9—14 gives another glimpse of Gideon's need and God's provision. What extraordinary scene transpires?

Then, in verses 15—18 we read the results of God's encouragement. Remember Gideon's conversation with the Angel in chapter 6? Gideon had questioned God's goodness. "If the LORD is with us," he said, "then why is all this happening?" Gideon began to see that God was indeed with them.

In Judges 6:24 Gideon had built an altar to the Lord and called it The LORD is peace. "Gideon experienced this name of God, Jehovah Shalom, when he experienced God's presence…Peace is bigger than calm. The word *shalom* means wholeness, completeness, well-being, having things properly aligned and ordered—no more drama, harmony, and balance."[17] This early recognition of God was reinforced over and over for Gideon. His testimony is for us to grab on to as well.

Moving on into Judges 7:19—22, look at the account of how the enemy was routed when God's strategy was used. Without having to use their swords, the Israelite band of 300 unleashed the judgment of heaven against the encamped Midianites. Then, the reinforcements from the tribes of Israel were called to action to pursue, capture, and to put to death the two leaders of the Midianite army: Oreb and Zeeb. What do we know about these two men?

Not much is stated, but there are clues in the meaning of their names. Oreb means raven. What does a raven do? By definition a raven, "1. Plunders, 2. Prowls for food, 3. Eats or feeds greedily or 4. Pillages."[18] We already read the incredible creativity in the ways Midian devoured Israel. Zeeb means wolf. The wolf characteristically gleans the stragglers, the weak, the young, or the defenseless from a herd or flock. So often we see this kind of behavior in families. The very place where nurture and safety should be, becomes the place of the most devastation. Those two men led the Midianite armies, directing the greedy devouring and ravaging of the land and the population.

Judges 8 begins with three scenes where Gideon's leadership was challenged within the House of Israel. For each, summarize the issue and Gideon's response to it.

1. Judges 8:1—3
2. Judges 8:4—7
3. Judges 8:8—9

In spite of the issues in the army and in the towns, Gideon managed to rout the rest of the Midianite army and capture the two kings, Zeba and Zalmunna. Just as with Oreb and Zeeb, the meanings of these two names bear significantly in this whole Midianite strategy. Zeba means "sacrifice"[19] or deprived of the protection from being sacrificed, as we learned it. Zalmunna means "protection refused"[20] –presumably the protection of something, like shade. Just think about the significance of these two kings coming year after year for seven years for the express purpose of stealing Israel's livelihood and ravaging the land and its people. In the end, these kings lost the protections they had denied Israel.

Judges 8:21—28 brings us to the end of the Midianite oppression. Does the story end well? What do you make of it?

The Redemptive Gift of Giving

We could subtitle this section, Stewardship vs Ownership, but let's start from the simplest common definition of give. To give is to transfer ownership of something from one person to another. Most often we probably think of it as voluntary rather than mandatory. Society generally has great appreciation for the generous, philanthropic types among us. Giving, then, is seen as good.

The Bible has a great deal to say about giving, and offers numerous examples of blessing that comes from giving. A Midianite priest gave shelter, employment, then a daughter to be wife to Moses. During Moses's sojourn in Midian, God was able to instill in him the heart and skills of a shepherd. Abigail brought gifts of food to David and his men in recognition of their protection, and in turn, saved David from the sin of vengeance. Her own household was spared from destruction. In 1 Kings 17 we see the story of the widow of Zarephath, who gave the prophet Elijah what she thought would be her last meal, and was blessed in return, with sufficiency throughout the three years of drought.

Jesus taught many lessons about giving. First, He taught about what priority our riches were to have in our lives (Matthew 6). In the encounter with the rich young ruler, Mark 10, Jesus urged him to exchange his earthly treasure for heavenly—give away the wealth to poor and needy and receive true, eternal riches. Luke's account of the Sermon on the Mount includes some profound instructions about giving. In Luke 6:30 Jesus tells us to give to everyone who asks for something from us. Just a few verses later we read "Give and it shall be given unto you: good measure, pressed down, shaken together, and running over will be put into your bosom. For with the same measure that you use, it will be measured back to you (Luke 6:38, NKJV)." These are just a few instances where Jesus talked about giving. The disciples got the message.

In Acts 4:35 we read of the earliest believers giving as anyone in the new emerging church had need. The material substance of life was not all they gave. Remember when Peter and John went to the temple to pray and met the lame man on the way? When asked for alms, Peter replied that they had no money, but they surely would give what they had—healing, in the Name of Jesus. The apostle Paul wrote three chapters in the second letter to the Corinthian believers exhorting them about a gift promised and its power to inspire others, of the necessity of following through on the promise with joy, not obligation, and of the extraordinary generosity of God to make sure that we always have enough to be able to give something in every situation. Then, just before the end of the scriptures, I John 3: 16—18 instructs us that our loving response to a brother or sister in need must be to give.

Lest we think that giving was optional in the Biblical teachings, it is good to look at the strong words in James 4:1—4. Here James gives us a good perspective on where looking out for self leads. Focusing on ourselves, our wants, needs, or fantasies leads to what?

What distinguishes the redemptive gift of giving from the general requirement God has established as the norm for His children? In the list of redemptive gifts in Romans 12:8 Paul wrote that "he who gives, give with liberality." The Greek word for give is *metadidomi*. It is the same word translated "impart" in Romans 1:11 where Paul is hoping to come to the believers in Rome "that I may impart to you some spiritual gift that you may be established." Romans 15:29 and 1 Corinthians 1:7 use the same term. This seems to indicate God-enabled resources given in such a way as to establish, stabilize, or position another person to be able to grow and mature in their faith. If we think about the good seed God sowed in us before we were even born, it is safe to hope that such spirit empowered giving is meant to free a person to be able to pursue his/her birthright. This is best understood in terms of stewardship. Stewardship can be defined as using one person's resources to accomplish another person's agenda. This is easily seen in an employer/employee relationship. It is also the fundamental principle in Kingdom economics. We, the children of God, use God's abundant resources to accomplish His amazing purposes, see John 3:34—36, Matthew 6:1—4 or Mark 12:1—12.

In contrast, ownership claims resources for oneself and uses them for one's own purposes. All of us tend to feel a right to what we think we have earned, built, discovered, etc. Some even feel entitled to things they have not earned, built, or discovered. What we own we protect. We determine how it will be used and who will share in it. Ownership, as a mindset, makes giving very difficult. It is not the model Jesus espoused. God calls us to walk "at risk" so that we must depend on His resources rather than on the natural resources we can utilize.

For the redemptive gift of giving, the Giver seems to naturally know how to give strategically. Typically givers excel in accumulating the particular resources which God intends for them to give: money, property, connections, etc. Godly giving carefully stewards those resources for the good of the recipients and to the glory of God. When the giver's sense of identity is tied to their gifts, a lie distorts the purpose of the gift. I, the giver, need to give and have the people who receive from me to affirm that I am a giver. This tends to make one prone to control the gift, or to give with strings attached. In a worst case scenario, the giver creates an unhealthy dependence upon themselves for some resource or another, which in turn serves his, the giver's, identity needs. God has established giving with a universal divine reciprocity; we only need to give as freely as we have received from His hand.

What Did Jesus Do?

Let's look at John 9, the miracle in which Jesus restored sight to a man born blind. Note the disciples' question concerning the source of the man's blindness (John 9:2). It was a commonly held belief that all deformity was a direct result of someone's sin, so the origin question was a natural one to ask. Jesus's answer turns that assumption on its ear. "Neither," He said. The explanation that follows points us to God's true ways, which bring light and life (See verses 4—5). Jesus spoke in terms of we; "We must do the work of HIM who sent Me." Immediately, we can connect with the idea of partnership with God. Jesus did not say that the man's blindness was so that Jesus could display His power to heal. Nor did He turn away from the impossibility of the man's congenital blindness to save Himself the trouble He must have anticipated would follow. It was, after all, the Sabbath.

The manner of Jesus's encounter with this blind man also demonstrates the ideal for the "giver." John 9: 6—7a tells us what Jesus actually did. Read this passage, then summarize it in your own words.

Jesus's actions, along with His instructions, effectively launched the blind man into his healing. They administer something without creating a dependence on Jesus. Jesus did not even instruct him to return after washing. The man's obedience brought about the healing God had intended to show forth His glory. Jesus's risk paid off. Later, after the healed man had been interrogated and thrown out of the Temple for having the audacity to claim his healing was of God, Jesus sought him out. The interview in verses 35—39 provides a forum for this man to discover his Healer-Messiah and make an informed choice about Jesus. What is the man's response in verse 38?

Remember that Jesus had said at the outset of this account that, "While I am in the world, I am the Light of the world." In the concluding scene Jesus distinguishes between physical and spiritual blindness, then redirects the question of whose sin is responsible. He has given healing, light, revelation, and choice to everyone involved with no strings attached. In every scene there was opportunity for truth and life to triumph. Later, in the book of Acts, we see that the disciples took the lesson to heart. Peter and John gave "such as [they] had" in the Name of Jesus and a lame man leaped for joy.

Application Points

1. The <u>cause</u> for God sending the Midianites against Israel was her sin.
2. The <u>generational sins</u> that opened the door for this curse:
   * When we make "soft" choices to keep ourselves comfortable, denying God's promise and/or calling;
   * When we choose comfort at the expense of the Kingdom;
   * When we create dependence or control others for what we can provide;
   * When we follow our own agenda without risk.

3. <u>Markers</u>: The principle marker of the Midianite curse is the existence of a seasonal pattern of devouring, predictable, possibly variable in the manner of devouring, but always devastating in its results, (remember Oreb and Zeeb). Recurrence is the key. A second marker is remarkably Zeeb-like. Devouring focuses on relationships, particularly in the family, where God intends life and blessing to flow. Holidays and significant events serve as the setting for both external disasters and consistent negative family dynamics to destroy the celebration.

4. <u>Redemptive gift</u>: The gift of giving takes the amazing capacity to generate some kind of wealth and leverage it for the purposes of God at His direction and for His glory concerning the needs of others.

5. <u>Legitimacy lie</u>: I am legitimate when I can provide the resources for others to do x-y-z.

6. <u>Blessing</u>: When this curse is broken: the very season of devouring becomes the season of greatest blessing. Resources start to work for you so that with God's timing and orchestration, your small investment is leveraged to something much greater than your efforts alone could produce to impact the next generation.

Prayer of Renunciation and Cleansing

Most Holy God, may Your Name be honored in all my worship and in all my living. Every good and perfect gift is from You. You alone are the creator of all that is. By Your breath life was given and by Your will and purpose it is sustained. It was Your good pleasure to create man in Your likeness and image, and to give him dominion—stewardship—over all You had made. Essential to successful stewardship was an intimate relationship with You, the Abba. You created us with freedom to choose a love relationship with You or life apart from You. Through Adam's sin dominion was relinquished to Satan and relationship with You was broken. All of creation came under the curse of sin. But You, O God, You provided a way of restoration through Your own begotten Son, Jesus. Jesus's extravagant love embraced us through the Cross and His blood has paid the price of our redemption. What a gift! What grace!

As I have looked into the gift of Your written word, I have learned about this Midianite curse which is transmitted generationally. I ask You to open the books for my life and for all my family lines. I acknowledge that it is Your intent that all of us walk in faithful stewardship of the gifts You give and the resources You provide for Your Kingdom purposes on earth, as in Heaven. I repent of my sin and the sin in my family lines that has brought this Midianite curse upon us. Specifically, I reject and renounce:

- That spirit of control, ownership, and faithlessness that has diverted my attention and goals from possessing my God-given birthright;
- The goal of maintaining comfort and security by my own efforts;
- The deception of postponing my birthright until a more convenient time;
- The sin of giving gifts with strings attached;
- The distrust of Your goodness;
- The running ahead of Your timing or lagging behind Your timing;
- The choice to live in fear instead of Your power, love, and sound thinking.

Furthermore, I agree with You for the breaking of every dedication of land, social or civic institutions, and covenants made by myself and any of my ancestors that would keep the Midianite curse in effect in myself and my family.

Lord Jesus Christ, as I confess these sins, I bring them before You, asking for forgiveness and for the cleansing of Your Blood from this Midianite curse in all its forms. Render it null and void. This You have promised, in 1 John 1:9, so I receive it now for myself and all of my family line.

Having received Your forgiveness and cleansing, in the authority delegated to me as a child of the Most High God, I now revoke the welcome of any spiritual demonic forces and powers that have operated under the Midianite curse in me and my family. I command you to the feet of Jesus Christ, the King of kings and Lord of lords, subject to His absolute authority.

Now, I rededicate myself to LORD Jesus Christ with FATHER and HOLY SPIRIT, our triune GOD, LORD of the universe and all eternity, the only true GOD. In Your great mercy and love, I humbly ask that You fill all those places where these sins resided with the Holy Spirit. Help me to walk by the Spirit and not by the flesh. Help me live in faithfulness, seeking Your kingdom first. Sanctify the times and seasons appointed for me, my spouse, and my physical and spiritual seed. I call forth all the blessings that were held back by the Midianite curse, so that the fullness of Your purposes in me can be invested for the next generation.

Glorify Your Name in all the earth! In Jesus's Name, AMEN.

CHAPTER 7
Jotham's Curse
Weekly Readings

Day 1: Read Judges 8:33—9:57.

Jot down key events and ideas from the passage. Include any insights you may have relevant to birthright, inheritance or generational sin.

Day 2: Read Exodus 28.

What stands out to you in these directions for priestly garments?

What do the priestly garments signify in terms of the situation in Shechem? (Judges 9)

Day 3: Today read Genesis 12:6; Genesis 33:18; Genesis 34.

What significant events in Israel's history took place in Shechem?

Day 4: Read Genesis 35:4; Joshua 24:32; Deuteronomy 11:26—32.

In the first two passages, what significant events transpire?

Then, in the passage from Deuteronomy, what role does Shechem have?

Day 5: Read John 11 and John 19:30.

Look for instances where the principles of covenant, honor, and gratitude are exhibited or denied.

Day 6: The parallel redemptive gift to Jotham's curse is leadership. Read from the following passages what the Bible says about leadership. Romans 12:8, Proverbs 29, Proverbs 30:21—22, Luke 22:26, 1 Timothy 3:1—13, Titus 1:5—9.

Jotham's Curse

This curse is, in many ways, the strangest of the curses. It has no appointed judge. There is no outside group that oppresses Israel. And, as in a true Shakespearean tragedy, the main characters die and the rest go home. So, to understand this curse, we will look back to the end of the leadership of Gideon, search back through some of Israel's history, examine the parallel redemptive gift of leadership with regard to its role in this curse, and study the passage in Judges.

First, a look back to Judges 8. After the glorious victory over the Midianites, remember that the men of Israel went to Gideon to invite him to become king over them (Judges 8:22–28). Gideon wisely declined the offer, stating that only God is worthy to be king over Israel. Later, he must have had some regret about the lack of tangible affirmation because he asked for donations of gold ornaments and jewelry from all the spoils of war which he then used to make an ephod, (the Day 2 reading in Exodus 28 describes an ephod and its purpose). Gideon then enshrined the ephod in his city. The Scripture says it became an idol and a snare to the people and to Gideon. What evidence do you find in Judges 8:33—9:57 that indicates that the golden ephod was a snare? To whom was it a snare?

Besides the ephod itself, Gideon also acquired other possessions, among them wives and sons. Judges 8:29—31 introduces us to the family. What does this tell us?

Had Gideon only given lip-service to God's Kingship? We cannot really judge, but the fruit at least calls forth the question. Think about popularity—the approval of men, issues of stewardship vs ownership, and violation of boundaries. How do these ideas come into play here?

With Jotham's curse we do not have a particular outside group afflicting Israel under God's judgment of her sin. Rather, we see a generational problem in Gideon's family and the society at large which translates to covenant violation, ingratitude, and dishonor. God allowed Israel the consequences of her sin.

The city of Shechem plays a prominent role in the whole history of Israel, not just this situation in Judges 9. Not only was Shechem the birthplace of the main character, Abimelech, it was also the first place Abram settled when he left Ur at God's instruction to go to the land God would provide (Genesis 12:6). Later, when Jacob returned to his homeland he purchased a piece of land from a man called Hamor (Genesis 33:18). Hamor's son, Shechem, dishonored Jacob's daughter by raping her, which set in motion a whole tragic saga of conniving, vengeance, deceit, and death. Shechem, the man, died in Shechem the city. Soon after that horrible event, Jacob called his whole clan to put away their foreign gods. When he collected the idols, he buried them at Shechem in an act of rededication to Jehovah. Joseph's bones, carried out of Egypt by his descendants, were buried at Shechem (Joshua 24:32). In Deuteronomy 11:26—32 we read God's reminder to the Israelites of their calling and the covenant between them that had begun with Abraham and been reaffirmed with each generation, both of which happened at Shechem. Shechem is situated in the shadow of both Mount Gerazim and Mount Ebal—mountains God used to role-play Blessing and Cursing (Deuteronomy 11). It is from Mount Gerazim, in Judges 9, that Jotham pronounces his curse upon Abimelech and the people of Shechem.

What had just happened in Shechem? See Judges 8:33 and 9:1—4.

In previous encounters in Judges, the Scripture tells us that the people turned aside and served the Baals/other gods. Here, in Judges 8 and 9, we notice a new name, Baal-berith. This was altogether new. The name itself indicates that Israel was not only adding idolatry to the worship of Jehovah, they were completely breaking the covenant and replacing Yahweh with this Baal-berith alone.

Another piece of history we would do well to consider carefully as we look at Israel is our own contemporary culture. Remember the spiraling degradation we looked at in both Romans 1 through 2 and in Judges 2? Paul wrote to the Romans that God gave mankind over to degrading lusts and passions. The summary statements in Judges 2 clearly declare that with each new rebellion against God, Israel became even more corrupt. Why should it be any different for us? Though many sense that something might be wrong in our present society, few seem to have any clear notion of what that is, nor how we have arrived at this place. The capacity to connect choices, values, and consequences has become nonexistent in the society at large. Even in the Church, we prefer personal comfort and encouragement over obedience and righteousness. We need to heed the old adage that warns that when we fail to learn from history, we are bound to repeat it. (It seems that more often, the negative consequences of history get repeated, not the positive advances!)

Abimelech's Conspiracy

Now, let's look at Abimelech. He was born in Shechem, son of Jerubaal, Gideon, and a concubine (Judges 8:31). A concubine could have been a wife or mistress. Regardless of marital status, she was considered second class at best. In this account she obviously is not even living with Gideon. Her name is never mentioned. What do you suppose was the impact of all this on Abimelech growing up?

Did he have a right to feel this way? Do you see any similarities with children growing up in our culture as a result of abandonment and rejection issues?

What did Abimelech do with his anger, rejection, bitterness, resentment, jealousy, betrayal, loneliness, hatred, etc.? Judges 9:1—6 paints a pretty gruesome picture.

Then the men of Shechem made Abimelech king. Jotham, the only half-brother who escaped being sacrificed on the same stone as his brothers, took up the offense in a peculiar way. Judges 9:7—15 relates a story shouted from Mount Gerazim for God and everyone else to hear. What sense do you make of the story?

Scripture calls this pronouncement a curse. Two Hebrew words are used in the text for what Jotham said. *Kalallah:* is pronouncing a formula wishing evil or harm on someone. *Harrar:* to hem in with obstacles, to bind, to render powerless to resist. Now look again at what Jotham actually said at the end of his tale. There is a formulaic if-then declaration concerning both Abimelech's actions and the populace of Shechem. If Abimelech acted honorably and with gratitude toward Jerubaal, then he should be blessed by God. But, if he did not, then harm, in the form of fire, was called forth to consume him and the people who supported his actions. The obstacles, or confinement, in Jotham's word curse are placed squarely in God's hands—Jehovah's, not Baal-berith's. God would be judge of all that had taken place that brought Abimelech into kingship. When did God answer? How did He answer?

Think about the issue of Covenant versus contract. Both define benefits, rights, blessings, requirements, and consequences for violation, but the covenant only ends honorably in death, while the contract makes provision for termination of agreement. Jotham wished to curse Abimelech and Shechem. He invoked the issues of broken covenant, calling forth covenant penalties (death), which then empowered the curse in heaven, even if not on earth (Judges 8:22). The pivotal issue for Jotham was gratitude, or honor (Judges 9:17—18), which was due

Gideon for his leadership and sacrifice on Israel's behalf against the Midianites. When God ruled on Jotham's curse, He confirmed the agreement of Heaven that honor and gratitude had been grossly violated by both Abimelech's slaughter of his half-brothers and Shechem's cooperation with him, then veneration of him as king. Interesting, is it not, that God used another discontented usurper to overthrow Abimelech! From this whole incident we must also see that if we violate God's principles of gratitude and covenant, we invite judgment.

Another concept related to leadership, which we see at work in this Judges 9 account, is the significance of favor as opposed to favors. See Romans 13:8 where the Apostle Paul speaks about owing no man anything. Pure favor comes with no strings attached: gifts freely given without expectation or demand. Favors, on the other hand, can be called forth in future payment, or payback, like an IOU. This is totally different than covenant gratitude under God's moral law. Israel denied favor and honor to Gideon and his family, and by endorsing Abimelech, went so far as to dishonor him. The judgment God rendered against Shechem and Abimelech confirmed His values of covenant, loyalty, honor, and gratitude.

Redemptive Gift of Leader/Ruler

Different Bible translations will sometimes use alternate words to try to convey the meaning of a Hebrew or Greek term. The parallel redemptive gift for Jotham's curse, from Romans 12, has been translated both as ruler and leader. In English, the two words are not exactly the same. Webster defines a ruler as a "person who rules or governs; sovereign."[21] The word "rule" has twenty-two definitions. Here are a few of them, according to Webster: "1) a principle or regulation governing conduct, procedure, arrangement, etc., 2) control, government, dominion, 3) tenure of conduct of reign of office."[22] The definition of a leader is someone who leads. More specifically, to lead is "1) to go before or with to show the way, 2) to influence or induce, 3) to guide in direction, course, action, opinion, etc.; bring."[23]

As you may readily see, the two terms are not exactly the same in nature by definition. The ruler has more of an 'I-am-above-you' feel. The ruler dominates, sets the boundaries, and enforces them. The leader encourages and guides in the truth and integrity. The godly leader feels more like an 'I-am-with-you/let's-do-this-together" kind of person. As the original Biblical language has been thus translated both ways, it is safe to think that the definition encompasses both meanings. We see this combination in the role of parenting. We see it also in God's dealings with mankind. Both set boundaries, and both guide and direct according to what is best, (hopefully so, for parents, definitely for God). But, a person can be a bad leader/ruler. History, as well as our present world culture, give many examples of leadership. Abimelech was a leader. King David was a leader. Leaders are gifted by God to build organizations, even nations, which are life-giving, releasing other gifts into the earth realm. A gifted leader/ruler will recognize the vision those he/she leads are to embrace. There will be a calling out of the gifts, talents, strategies, and resources needed from the constituency in order to build upon that vision. Creativity, unity, honor, and gratitude are among the fruits of truly good leadership. From a spiritual perspective, they are also attributes of covenant, the primary mode of relationship established by God.

The problem with leaders or rulers is that they can be very gifted by God, but very broken as people. Like Abimelech, some people have a great capacity to get the cooperation of others to build a kingdom, or organization, or business. Like Abimelech, they also may resort to any number of lawless violations to attain their goals. Abimelech executed his half-brothers with the help of a mercenary band whom he hired with money donated from the pagan temple treasury. This is not leadership as God intends. There is no life in it. In fact, it costs life. The fundamental operating lie for Abimelech-style leadership is that his legitimacy is established by using his power to build his own little kingdom.

What Did Jesus Do?

When we read of the miracle of raising Lazarus from the dead in John 11, it is important to orient ourselves to the times surrounding that event. We learn in John 11:1 that Jesus's friend, Lazarus, was sick. A message from his sisters found Jesus with the disciples outside Judea. Just prior to this, at the winter Feast of Dedication in Jerusalem, Jesus had twice narrowly avoided being stoned by unbelieving Jewish leaders. Presumably, Jesus and the disciples had removed themselves to a quieter place where Jesus could continue preparing them for their destinies, which would commence with the fulfillment of His. Time was of the essence. The cross was imminent. As always for Jesus, being where the Father sent Him, doing what the Father commanded, and working in the Father's timing was imperative. Jesus received news from His friends, Martha and Mary, informing Him of beloved Lazarus's serious illness. What responses do we see from the disciples?

What does Jesus mean in verse 4, "This sickness is not unto death, but for the glory of God, that the Son of God may be glorified through it."?

What significance could there be in the two day delay?

What emotions do you perceive in the discussion between Jesus and the disciples in verses 7—16?

What happened to the whole notion of God's glory?

There are many excellent expositions of this record of the raising of Lazarus from the dead. Our purpose here is to look specifically at Jesus in the role of leader or ruler. Truth is central. Notice that it was the Jewish leaders' unbelief, despite Jesus's having spoken Truth to them, that brought their accusations and judgments. Conversely, Martha's choice to believe the One who is "the resurrection and the life" caused her to hope. In the same way, Mary received the Truth. The women's faith released Jesus to do what had awaited the proper time. We can hear in Jesus's prayer at the graveside the passionate desire that those who longed to believe in Him as Messiah would see it confirmed in the miracles He did. Then He commanded, "Lazarus, come forth," and, "Unwrap him." As leader, Jesus stayed in covenant with the twelve chosen disciples despite all their failings and all that tugged on His time and attention, even Judas's demons.

Jesus remained in covenant with Israel despite more "fruit" with the Gentiles to whom He ministered. Jesus never developed an institution in His lifetime to establish His legitimacy. Nor did He depend upon institutional approval for His agenda. The Establishment of His day responded vigorously against both Jesus and Lazarus because of this miracle. They considered them a threat to their own legitimacy, and so aggressively sought a way to put a stop to Jesus and His mission. Still, Jesus only did what God had called Him to do.

The next words of the seven last words of Jesus at the cross are, "It is finished (John 19:30, NIV)." There are two applications that fit our focus here. First, this is a declaration of the truth that the price for mankind's sin and rebellion is fully paid in Jesus's death. Second, it is an announcement that Jesus had finished the work God sent Him to do—not just kept busy filling His own agenda. The covenant commission from Heaven was fully executed on Jesus's part. He conquered through sacrifice; He won by losing all.

Like Jesus, we have authority over this curse when we are covenant keepers, when entitlement is not part of our motivation, and when we understand that it is God who determines whether we stay or go, what kind of fruit we see, and the movement or growth that comes through our obedience.

Application Points

1. The _cause_ of this curse was Israel's sin.
2. The <u>generational sin</u> that brings about this curse is when someone in the family line violated covenant relationship, like when Israel violated the debt of gratitude toward Gideon and his family. Sedition, lawlessness, ingratitude, and dishonor characterize the behaviors.
3. <u>Markers</u>: There is one principle marker with Jotham's curse: a pattern of internal division or breaking apart, often with significant loss of some sort of capital or resources. This manifests in organizations rather than simply acting on an individual, (_eg;_ The Azusa Street revival birthed the modern Pentecostal movement very powerfully. But when divisions formed, one group split away and moved to Washington, taking the whole mailing list with them. That was a significant loss of information resources).
4. <u>Redemptive gift</u>: The spiritual anointing for righteous, life-giving leadership/rulership released to build organizations and institutions that serve the vision well, as well as honoring individuals and keeping covenant.
5. <u>Legitimacy lie</u>: I am legitimate when I have institutional power to build. Abimelech sought his own legitimacy through ruling.
6. <u>Blessing</u> when the curse is broken: One is free to build social structures that are synergistically productive and life-giving to a culture. This encompasses business, government, nonprofits, families, schools, churches. It is possible to possess your birthright simply as an individual, but you can never be a person of destiny apart from community. It takes a social structure to nurture destiny.

Prayer of Renunciation and Cleansing

Almighty God and Heavenly Father, I praise You for being the source of true covenant and the only absolute covenant keeper. I acknowledge that You created man in Your image to be in relationship with You. I acknowledge that You saw that it was not good for man to be alone, so created woman, thus establishing the first social institution, a family. Therefore, I proclaim that You are the God of family, community, institutions, and governments. You have designed these human institutions to be life-giving, to be strategic, and generational. I praise You for the wisdom by which the universe is founded. You are good and all You do is good.

I confess that sin and poor choices have corrupted Your plan so that death, instead of life, is at work in all levels of society. I ask You to open the Books for all my generational lines. I confess, reject, and renounce the sins of ingratitude toward all who were life-givers to us. I confess as sin all covenant breaking wherever it is found. I confess, reject, and renounce the sins of sedition, of lawlessness, and any other sins that accompany covenant breaking. Judge of All, I repudiate the lie that legitimacy can come from having power through an institution. I reject and renounce that as sin in myself and my family line.

Father, as I have seen Jotham's curse in operation in my life and in our society, the death, destruction, and suffering it brings is painful. Yet, I acknowledge that You are just to allow the wages of sin, so I accept that judgment, but I also accept Jesus's redemptive sacrifice on my behalf and ask that in Your mercy, with these confessions, that Jesus's blood would cover every sin that brought about Jotham's curse in me and my family lines. In Your faithfulness, cleanse me, my spouse, and our physical and spiritual seed from every vestige of this curse.

I now revoke the welcome of any spiritual demonic force or power that acted in this curse. In the delegated authority I have as a child of God, in Jesus's name, I command every demonic entity that was empowered by this curse to leave me, my family, my ministry, my businesses, and all else connected to me. In the places where these powers operated, I ask that You fill me with Your Holy Spirit, Lord Jesus, producing fruit, teaching me how to walk in covenant with You, with my spouse, family, and with all the institutions where You place me.

I rededicate myself to You, Lord Jesus Christ, with FATHER and HOLY SPIRIT, our triune God, LORD of the universe and all eternity, the only true GOD. Teach me how to be a life-giver, even when others are covenant breakers. Give me grace to finish the course that You have laid out for me. I ask that You release the blessings that have been blocked by this curse so that I, and my family after me, can begin to walk out the destiny that is part of my inheritance.

Thank You, Jesus, because You did keep covenant and finished the course to the glory of the eternal God. In Your name I pray, Amen.

CHAPTER 8
The Ammonite Curse
Weekly Readings

Day 1: Read Judges 10:1—5 and Judges 12:8—15.

Before we actually look at the Ammonite curse we need to check out a few leaders who "ruled" in Israel but without an enemy to defeat.

How many leaders do you count in these passages?

Who were they?

What do you see as significant about their contributions to Israel's culture?

Day 2: Read Judges 10:6—12:7.

Summarize the essential points in this account of Israel's next judge.

What seems especially significant?

Day 3: Review the Genesis 13 and Genesis 19:30—38 story of Lot and the origin of the Ammonites.

What is the difference between the younger daughter's decision and the elder's?

Day 4: Read the following verses about mercy: Proverbs 11:17, Matthew 5:7, and Luke 18:13.

What do they say about mercy?

Day 5: Read Isaiah 63:9, Daniel 4:27 and Ephesians 2:4.

What more did you learn about mercy, its origin, and its value in God's eyes?

Day 6: First, read in John 21 the account of Jesus's last miracle.

What did Jesus do?

Now read Luke 23:46, Jesus's last words on the cross.

How is the mercy of God manifested in Jesus's words and actions in both passages?

Judges 10: the State of the Nation

When one of our Presidents gives a state of the union address, it is usually embellished with all kinds of wonderful examples of how much he has accomplished and what wonderful strides we have made as a people. Then, he will identify the challenges to be tackled in the year ahead, as well as the strategies he believes will resolve them, thereby making us all happier and better off under his leadership. As we turn to the next chapter of Israel's story in Judges, we have just finished seeing how a broken man, Abimelech, brought in great and destructive division. Chapter 10 presents a sort of state of the nation perspective on Israel. The first item we see is that instead of God raising up a judge, two different men "arose to save" Israel. First, Tola for 23 years. Then Jair, who judged for 22 years, and he had thirty sons who rode on thirty donkeys and, they had thirty cities in the land of Gilead. What does all that tell us about where their priorities were focused?

After these two guys were dead and gone, verse 6 tells us that Israel again did evil in the sight of the Lord. (Consider the meaning of the phrase 'in the sight of the Lord.' God sees everything, even that which we try to hide. In this phrase we see two powerful ideas: God's view of sin and the people's total indifference to what God said). It is very interesting that Judges 10 names a whole list of pagan gods that Israel had turned to, as if they were pursuing any and all gods except the God of covenant. They forsook the Lord, meaning they abandoned, left behind, omitted from thought, and completely replaced, Yahweh.

How was this different than the previous five judgments Israel faced?

Who were the nations to which God sold Israel?

How long were they oppressed?

Judges 10:10—16 gives us a glimpse of the confrontation between the Lord and Israel. Describe this exchange in your own words. What does it mean?

Verse 16 should just send shivers up and down your spine! No matter how far we have strayed, no matter how many other pursuits we have put in the place of God, no matter what or how many evil things we have participated in, when we turn from our wicked ways and seek the Lord, He has mercy on us. We looked at covenant in the last chapter. We are looking at mercy in this case. Notice how these two converge in Jesus, the cross, and His resurrection. Jesus said, "This is the new covenant in My blood (Luke 22:20)." He also said, "I did not come to abolish the Law or the prophets; I did not come to abolish but to fulfill (Matthew 5:17)." It was out of His love and mercy that He came to fulfill what?

If you answered Law, that would be correct in terms of the text but, it was something deeper; it was covenant. What did it look like to make a covenant? Look back in Genesis 15:6—21. This is the account of the covenant that God made with Abram. The amazing thing with Abram and God's covenant is that only God walked through the field of sacrifice. He was saying He was not only initiating this covenant, but was taking up the responsibility for both sides. Wow! Then, in John 3:16, we see, "For God so loved the world that He gave His only begotten Son, that whoever believes in Him should not perish, but have eternal life." Jesus became the Passover Lamb, without spot or blemish, who died to redeem us. God knew His people could not keep the Law. They would always fail. Jesus not only became our Redeemer paying the wages of sin, He also ushered in the New Covenant whereby we can live through the power of His resurrection and with His Spirit indwelling us.

Israel's condition here in Judges 10 is nothing like one of our state of the union addresses. It was not a pretty picture, but God, in mercy moved on Israel's behalf. We need to note one other piece before we look at how God moved. Back in verse seven, it was both Ammon and the Philistines into whose hands they were sold. Only the Ammonites are dealt with here. This is the second time we see something of the Philistines. Have you thought of any possible explanation?

The Ammonites

You will recall the Genesis 19 passage from our study of the Moabite curse. Ben-Ammi was the son of Lot by his younger daughter. Genesis 19:38 says that "He is the father of the Ammonites to this day." Remember that Lot had joined Abram and Sarai when they left Ur in Chaldea for a new land. Lot had stayed with Abram and prospered with him until their herds and flocks grew so large that quarrelling broke out between the herdsmen. The solution was to separate, with one going eastward, and the other west. In an extraordinarily generous gesture, Abram actually deferred to Lot's preference for the lush, well-developed land to the east. God blessed both men. Abram knew the promise of God that all the land would be his inheritance, so he acted generously toward Lot, but it is reasonable to ask what explanation Lot had.

What choices did Lot make, as indicated in the text of Genesis 19, both while resident in Sodom and later, when he holed up in the cave?

What choices did the daughters make to compensate for Lot's failure concerning them?

What is the significant difference between the older daughter's actions and the younger daughter's?

How hard is it to stand up for what is right, especially when there are good arguments and pressures to do otherwise? Or, when the one presenting an alternative option is stronger or older, an authority, or a relative? How many times do we go along so we do not upset the apple cart?

It is amazing how children in the same family, in the same circumstances, can have such different outcomes. Boundary issues are the same in this curse as they were for the Moabite curse. However, the biggest impact with the youngest daughter came because of her inability to see her own value and trust God for her future. Doing what was right was sacrificed to the choice to go along with her sister's plan. What other choices might the girls have made?

This was the beginning of the Ammonites. If you look at a map of the ancient Middle East you will find Ammon located just north of Moab, and east of the Jordan River in Israel. "The Ammonites were responsible for human sacrifice to Molech."[24] It was into their hands that the Lord sold Israel. Remember also that Ammon was allied with the Philistines, whom we have encountered earlier in Judges with the Moabites. It is interesting that we usually encounter the Philistines and the Ammonites in company with other nations!

A Closer Look: Judges 10:17—12:7

Starting at Judges 10:17, we find the people of Israel gathered at Gilead in an intense discussion. What is the concerning issue?

Why do you suppose the elders of Israel were unwilling to lead?

Enter Jephthah. Judges 11:1—3 introduces him to us. Who was he? What set him apart?

That passage, Judges 11:1—3, actually took place before 10:18. The story continues in chapter 11:4 with, "Sometime later…" Jephthah had been chosen to be Israel's military hope against the Ammonites. What do we learn about Jephthah in his response to the elders' "invitation"?

Does it seem like the elders tried to sweeten the deal by offering Jephthah more than just military leadership? See verse 11:8. Why?

Jephthah took the offer. Think about the ideas of birthright, inheritance, and destiny in terms of Jephthah. What characteristics manifest God's possible purpose for him?

What circumstances had adversely affected fulfillment of that purpose?

Ask yourself, how did he become a valiant warrior? How did his birth circumstances affect outcome? What kinds of feelings did he probably have? What made worthless fellows gather around him? Did the choices that he made help him become all that God intended? Without explicit information, our ideas concerning all these questions are conjecture. However, they are important to ponder because the human condition has not changed.

Once the Elders' commission was accepted, and after the people officially made Jephthah head over Israel, he immediately sent a message to the king of Ammon. This exchange is in Judges 11:12—28. What do you find intriguing about this? What was the purpose?

What was the outcome of Jephthah's diplomatic overtures?

In verses 29—40 we find Jephthah subduing the Ammonites. It would seem like a victory, and in so far as the Ammonites were concerned, it was; but therein was also a tragedy. What was the tragedy?

Then, in 12:1—7, we read of yet another tragedy. What was this one?

What are the similarities with the record of Gideon's conquest of the Midianites?

What are the differences between the two?

The retort in the last half of Judges 12:4 must have sounded like old "tapes" to Jephthah. The ensuing slaughter of kinsmen repeated on a much larger scale the tremendous losses

Jephthah had already experienced from his half-brothers and the sacrifice of his own daughter at his hand. It is enough to make us cry out for mercy. Mercy!

Mercy, the Parallel Redemptive Gift

The issue for Israel then was the same as it is for us. Will we follow our way, the world's way or way of the flesh, or God's way? First, let's scroll through the Jephthah account to see where mercy might have been demonstrated. Then we will look at what mercy means through some related Bible passages.

At first glance, mercy was decidedly lacking in this account of Jephthah. It wasn't demonstrated by the Ephraimites and it was not demonstrated in Jephthah's response to the men of Ephraim. If we go back farther, we see that Ammon did not show the Israelites mercy when they came out of Egypt on their way back to the Promised Land. Even farther back, we saw in the beginnings of the Ammonites that Lot did not show mercy to his girls in Sodom, though they survived destruction because of God's mercy.

God was the only one who demonstrated true mercy; first, to the people of Israel by relenting from His anger and coming to their aid and, secondly, by filling Jephthah with His Spirit to enable him to prevail against the Ammonites. Remember the beginning of the account of Jephthah in Judges 10:6—14? When Israel cried out to God for help, the Lord essentially told them to forget it. "Go and cry out to the gods you have chosen," He said. Israel responded to the Lord's rebuke in verse 15. What was that response?

Then, Judges 10:16 relates God's mercy. What does the text say was God's response to Israel?

Later, after the elders of Israel had had to eat humble pie and go ask Jephthah for help, and after Jephthah had negotiated for the honor of "headship" in the event of victory, we see the mercy of God at work in Jephthah. How might his initial communication to the King of Ammon have been an attempt to show mercy? Did it work?

Then, in Judges 11:29, "The Spirit of the Lord came upon Jephthah," so that victory was assured. How did Jephthah respond to that mercy of God?

Have you ever tried to buy God's favor? Think about it.

What does mercy mean? According to *Webster's Ninth Collegiate Dictionary*, mercy means: 1) Compassionate or kindly forbearance shown toward an offender, an enemy, or other person in one's power, 2) the disposition or discretionary power to be compassionate or forbearing, 3) an act of kindness, compassion, or favor, and 4) something of good fortune; blessing. The word grace is similar. One of its meanings is mercy. It also means unmerited favor. It was at the cross that mercy and justice came together. "It is for freedom that Christ set us free (Galatians 5:1, NIV)." God continues to demonstrate His mercy toward us.

We looked at Micah 6:8 at the beginning of the course, let's look at it again now. "What does the Lord require of you, but to do justly, to love mercy, and to walk humbly with your God." We can only do that by walking in the Spirit. Further down, in Galatians 5:13—26, we get a good picture of what it does not look like to walk in the Spirit. In 1 John 2:15—17 we find "the lust of the flesh, the lust of the eyes and the boastful pride of life." These things are "all that is in the world." We might even say that these are the opposites of doing justly, loving mercy, and walking humbly with our God. The lust of the flesh is gratifying physical desires. The lust of the eyes means satisfying soul desires—craving what we see. The boastful pride of life is the self-sufficiency, doing things our way, in our own strength, and drawing attention and credit to ourselves. Being others-centered, justice, mercy, and God-centered, and walking humbly with God, are the priorities God has established. Jesus put it this way when asked which was the greatest commandment, "Love the Lord your God with all your heart, soul, and mind. . .and love your neighbor as yourself (Matthew 22:36—39, NIV)." Then, He added that all the Law and the Prophetic writings were wrapped up in these two commands. It is the same struggle for us today that it was then.

The gift of mercy flows from the heart of God. It is more emotion-driven, intuitive, creative, and intimate, both in its perspective and manifestations. As a result, the mercy-bearer is often in conflict with their culture. Very often their own pain, like Jephthah's, becomes the springboard for mercy to others. Jephthah did not do very well with mercy. However, God's mercy is evident in several areas: the obvious call and anointing to be a valiant warrior, the redemption of the time of his exile to hone those skills, the empowering of Holy Spirit for victory, and the elders' recognition of Jephthah's real qualifications. 2 Corinthians 1 is the Apostle Paul's teaching about comfort, which can easily be a model for mercy at work in the Body of Christ. That which we have received from God in our own need, becomes the well of mercy for others.

What Did Jesus Do?

What did Jesus do? Though born with the stigma of questionable birth and the stigma of coming from Nazareth, Jesus walked in who He was and rejected the attempts of people to define Him. Jesus lived out of the Father's declaration over Him, "This is MY beloved Son, in whom I am well pleased (Matthew 3:17, NKJV)." Jesus refused to embrace the traditions of men, or the corruptions of men, in order to keep peace. Throughout His entire ministry Jesus was undeterred from pursuing His birthright, which was to be the Savior of the world. In the triumph of the cross and His resurrection, Jesus received from the Father the full compensation for His obedience. Philippians 2:9—11 declares His supremacy.

Let's look at John 21. The setting was shortly after Jesus's resurrection. Several of the disciples had gone to the Sea of Galilee. What do you imagine was going through their minds?

Peter, apparently uneasy with waiting around, initiated a fishing trip. Who knows what his intentions were, but the others volunteered to go along. All night fishing with no fish in the nets by morning must have felt pretty bad on top of all the uncertainties in their minds. Jesus knew where they were and what they were doing. He met them that morning. From the shore He offered a word of advice, "Drop your nets on the other side." This resulted in a miraculous catch of fish. That was a mercy after a fruitless night for the fishermen. Even better was the joyous recognition that it was Jesus waiting for them on the shore.

Later, over a hearty breakfast, Jesus drew Peter aside. The whole private conversation is a picture of mercy—God's heart for both Peter and the world Peter was destined to impact. Peter had denied Jesus three times during His interrogation before Caiphas. Three times Jesus gave him opportunity to refute those denials. Peter had turned back to fishing, the thing he knew, when uncertainties weighed heavily upon his heart. When fishing failed, Jesus had provided a miraculous catch. Then Jesus redirected Peter from what Peter could do to what God would have him do. "Feed My lambs, Shepherd My sheep, and Feed My sheep." With each affirmation of Peter's love for Jesus, Jesus drew Peter deeper into the mercy of His forgiveness, love, restoration, and commission. Then, Jesus shared a picture of how Peter's life would end. There would be radical sacrifice for Christ, even the fulfillment of Peter's earlier declaration that he would die for Christ, but it was not to buy the forgiveness and love Peter needed. That was already given. Peter would be able to shepherd the flock of Jesus Christ secure in the love of God because of the mercy poured out right there around the campfire on the seashore.

Jesus's love and sacrifice triumphed for us all because it was empowered by the passion of the Father's heart. "Mercy triumphs over judgment (James 2:13b, NASB)."

Application Points

1. The <u>cause</u> for the Ammonite curse was Israel's sin.

2. The <u>generational sin</u> which is carried in the Ammonite curse enters when you or someone in your family line violates moral or civil law to buy (God's) favor, or appease God through radical sacrifice. A primary opening for that sin is one's inability to receive God's valuation of one's self, then live out of that revelation. An intermediate cause can be where individuals violate moral or civil law so as not to offend another person, as in the case of Lot's younger daughter. In all of these, God is reduced to a formula which a person can fill by his own actions, thereby attempting to manipulate God or force God to conform to human will.

3. <u>Markers</u>: Like the Moabite curse, the Ammonite curse is marked by regular violations of boundaries, particularly in areas related to time. "Sometime later…" in Judges 11 is very telling. The principle, most devastating marker is barrenness—no fruit, which can be in the realm of physical, spiritual, business, education, etc. Jephthah's vow cost him his inheritance. Without the daughter, there was no one to carry forward the gifts and callings God intended to flow in the bloodline from generation to generation. Jephthah robbed himself of great fruitfulness and blessing. This curse can be corporate. It is marked by the wholesale defense of individuals at the expense of the community, resulting in large capitol lost and defilement of the creative gifts and ministries of compassion.

4. <u>Redemptive gift</u>: Mercy is that Spirit-given capacity to unselfishly, even sacrificially, pour the love of God into the deep wounds of persons and cultures.

5. <u>Legitimacy lie</u>: I am legitimate when I have earned favor, especially God's favor, through personal efforts and radical self-sacrifice. The shift from operating in the gift of mercy to operating out of this lie is principally a change in focus from being centered in the heart of God for others to being driven to "earn" God's heart for myself. There is a fundamental belief that one must earn or buy God's love through radical service/sacrifice.

6. <u>Blessing:</u> When the Ammonite curse is broken off and cleansed, God partners with you to help you possess your birthright. God's favor is infinitely greater than the work per se.

Prayer of Renunciation and Cleansing

Almighty God and Father, I rejoice that You are *Abba*. I rejoice that You desire an intimate relationship with me so much that You sent Your only Son to become my Redeemer. I praise You, Father, Son, and Holy Spirit for this great mercy.

I confess that I do not understand the depths and heights of that love. I have defined You by my experiences with my fellow man—the judgments, the slander, the punishment, and the ways we abuse each other. Foolishly, I have believed the lie that You are like us. As a result, I have made many choices based on that lie.

Lord, open the books of my family lines and shine Your light on them. I reject and renounce the lie that I need to, or that I can, earn Your favor or Your love. I reject and renounce the focus on human favor as well as the iniquity of valuing that favor more than even my birthright. I reject and renounce perfectionism, for it arises out of pride and a false confidence in my sufficiency. I reject and renounce every incident where someone chose to embrace human perspective instead of Your perspective. I reject every human stigma and pigeon-holing that is contrary to Your view. I reject and renounce the cultural pressure that calls me not to excel or choose what is right, lest I cause others to look bad. I reject and renounce the cowardice of failing to speak up about things that are evil lest I offend those around me. I ask You to forgive me and all in my family lines of all these iniquities and to cleanse me of all this unrighteousness. I plead the Blood of Jesus over my family lines, myself, my spouse, and my physical and spiritual seed. Furthermore, I revoke the welcome of any spiritual-demonic-forces and powers that operated in or over this Ammonite curse. With the delegated authority that is mine in Christ Jesus, I command every devouring spirit that has been empowered by this curse to leave me, my spouse, and my physical and spiritual seed now, and to never return.

I now rededicate myself to the LORD Jesus Christ with Father and Holy Spirit, our triune God, Lord of the universe and all eternity, the only true God. Fill me afresh with the spirit of wisdom and revelation in the knowledge of Christ, so that I may know You more. Help me to press on in the quest to lay hold of that for which You, God, laid hold of me in Christ Jesus. Thank You for redeeming me because You loved me, not because I earned Your love. I love You, Lord. Be glorified even in my life. All glory, honor, blessing, and praise be Yours now and forever. Amen and amen.

CHAPTER 9
The Philistine Curse
Weekly Readings

Day 1: Read Judges 13—16, the story of Samson. Note: remember that we have already encountered the Philistines twice before in Judges.

What insights do you gain in this account?

What questions arise from this story?

Day 2: Read 1 Samuel 13, focusing on verses 19—22.

What do you see here about the way the Philistines related to Israel?

Did their strategy work? How?

Day 3: Read 1 Samuel 17.

What was unusual about this battle plan?

Why was it an effective means to victory?

Day 4: Read Genesis 21:22—34 and Genesis 26:12—35.

What is the origin of a generational sin in this passage?

With whom is it manifest?

Day 5: Read John 5:1—15.

What did Jesus do to meet the man's need?

Next read John 19:28—29. What does Jesus's cry, "I thirst," reveal to us?

Day 6: Read these passages that speak about the importance of teaching: Deuteronomy 6:1—9; Isaiah 30:19—21; Psalm 25:4—5; Luke 12:12 and Matthew 10:24-25. Remember Judges 2:10.

Why was this Israel's condition?

Who Were the Philistines?

The first mention of the Philistines in the Bible is in Genesis 10 in the list of descendants of Noah after the world-wide flood. We have already visited this account when we investigated the origin of the Canaanites. It is fascinating to think that we are all Noah's progeny. Contemporary historians have traced people groups alive today back to individuals in this chapter. For example, one of the sons of Japheth, Magog, is ancestor to the Russian people, who are prophesied in Ezekiel 38 and 39 concerning the last days—the ones we are living now! It is in this context that we find the first mention of the Philistines.

Genesis 10:13 & 14 tell us that Ham's second son, Mizraim, had several sons. The second to last in the list is "Casluhim, from whom came the Philistines." Secular and Biblical historians are not clear on the exact place the Philistines settled. Some called them the sea people, possibly from Greece and Crete. Others feel they settled somewhere in Egypt. Whether they came out of Egypt, or fought against Egypt and were rebuffed, what is clear is that at some point they migrated to the coastal region of the Promised Land.

The next appearance of the Philistines is in Genesis 20 & 21. Abraham is moving his household toward the land of the Negev where he settles in Gerar, the land of the Philistines. For the second time in the record of Abraham, he has his wife Sarah say she is his sister, presumably to protect him. The ploy does not work because the King of Gerar took Sarah into his house to become a "wife," but God prevented him from violating Sarah. God actually gave the king a dream which prompted Sarah's release. God instructed Abraham to intercede for the king and his household for a healing; God had closed all the wombs. It was during the time among the Philistines that Isaac was born. Hagar and Ishmael were driven away. At the end of Abraham's time among the Philistines, in Genesis 21:22, we learn a significant piece of history. Abimelech, the king, and Phicol, commander of the army, while speaking to Abraham, acknowledged that they could see that God was with Abraham in all that he did. They asked him to swear by God that he would not deal falsely with them. In other words, they wanted to make a covenant of peace. The scripture tells us that Abraham did just that. Was this right or wrong for Abraham? Explain your reason.

Isaac grew up, married Rebekah, a beauty like his own mother, and went to live amongst the Philistines because of a famine in the land, see Genesis 26:2. Isaac then settled in Gerar. God blessed him even in the midst of famine. Even so, Isaac tried to use the same deception his father had used, with very similar results. What did he do?

This is an example of how generational sin starts and continues. Had Isaac seen his father try this trick with King Abimelech?

Now look at Genesis 26:13—14. What did God's promised blessing to Isaac look like?

Verses 14 and 16 tell us the Philistines' reaction to Isaac's blessings. What was it?

What do you suppose was God's intention in placing Isaac in the middle of Philistine territory and blessing him, but not them?

Remember that God is not willing that any should perish! He wants all people to come to Him and be set free.

We do not see much more of the Philistines until the book of Judges—there are only brief mentions in Exodus and Joshua 13. The mention in Joshua is in the midst of the division of the Promised Land into parcels of inheritance; the five lords of the Philistines occupied some of the area God gave the Israelites. In Judges 3 the five lords of the Philistines are on the list of nations God left to test Israel, because of her disobedience. For other people groups only the name is mentioned: Canaanites, Sidonians, Hivites, etc. What is different or significant about the five lords of the Philistines?

Unique Considerations

The scripture is careful to give some unique distinctions in Israel's history with regard to the Philistines. Let's list some of the differences we see in the Philistine curse. We present them as questions without obvious answers, but think about them. Reach for what is not obvious. First, God's use of the Philistines to discipline Israel is not a single large oppression. They are mentioned twice before Samson comes on the scene to begin to deliver Israel. Why is that?

Secondly, the weapons used against the Philistines are out of the ordinary. Why?

And thirdly, there was no finality in any of these accounts in Judges. Why is that?

In fact, we encounter the Philistines in 1 Samuel 4—7, oppressing Israel again by stealing the Ark of the Covenant. Where did they take it and set it up?

How did that work out for the Philistines?

Then, Israel cried out for a king so they could be like other nations. After Saul was anointed king, from 1 Samuel 13 and onward, we read of constant warfare. What is the clue to all this in 1 Samuel 13:19—22?

Look at 1 Samuel 17. What weapon did David use against the Philistine giant, Goliath?

None of the other curses have these unique characteristics. These very distinctions give us insight in to how we are to deal with the Philistine curse today.

The Redemptive Gift of Teaching

What do you think is the most important element you can pass on to your children? What will constitute their inheritance?

Here are some scripture passages that are sure to give you the biblical perspective:

- Proverbs 1:5—9
- Proverbs 2:1—10
- Proverbs 9:19
- Psalm 111:10
- 1 Corinthians 1:18–31

What you teach will be the most important part of your children's inheritance. By definition, *teach* means: "to impart knowledge or skill in; give instruction in, (2) to impart knowledge or skill to; give instruction to"[25] –both the subject matter and the audience being important. Teaching happens through demonstration, discipline, and direct instruction. We tend to think that what is taught is true. But think, is that always the case? It does not take much to recognize "untruths" taught both historically and currently. What happens when information is withheld or manipulated? What happens to the people on the receiving end of such communications? Just think about the impact Hitler had in Germany with all his anti-Semitic propaganda!

Proverbs 29:18 says, "Without a vision the people perish, but happy is he who keeps the Law." This tells us that if what people receive is warped and twisted, they will not have good vision. It also tells us that there is more to information than just human understanding. That is a clue to one of the reasons unusual weapons were used against the Philistines. There is more to any situation than just what we can perceive with human senses; there is also the spiritual dimension. We need Godly wisdom for solutions. We need Godly strategies for situations. The Scriptures tell us to be led by the Spirit into all truth so that we will know the truth and the truth will set us free.

In the Day 2 readings in 1 Samuel 13:19—22 we got a glimpse of what the Philistines were doing. They were controlling knowledge of blacksmithing in order to force Israel to come to them for metal tools and their maintenance, but more significantly, to prevent Israel from making weapons for her own protection. Fear was certainly a motivating factor in this manipulation and control of vital, life-giving information. Why, you may ask, can we make such a claim? Look back to Genesis 26, the account of Isaac's sojourn among the Philistines during a time of famine in the land. Remember that God instructed Isaac to go to Gerar instead of Egypt, and with the instructions came a promise of blessing. God was faithful to His word. The Philistines witnessed an amazing multiplication of crops and herds in Isaac's household while their own suffered. They acknowledged that God was with Isaac, else such blessing could not have happened. However, instead of seeking knowledge of Isaac's God and favor from His hand, they protected themselves by sending Isaac away. The covenant with Isaac was insurance for the Philistines, but a curse for Isaac and his descendants.

Judges 13—16, Samson as Judge

One of the commands the Lord had Moses repeat often to the Israelites was that they were to be diligent to teach their children everything that they had learned about Yahweh. All day long, in all that they did, they were to teach. They were to teach by word and by action so that each generation would follow the Lord. On our way through Judges we have seen the decline in Israel's society in a number of ways. With the first four times of judgment and oppression, a judge was raised up, the oppressive nation was subdued, and a time of peace followed. We did not see this after Abimelech or Jephthah. Remember that both Abimelech and Jephthah grew up in broken home situations. In Judges 12, after Jephthah defeated the Ammonites, he fought with his own countrymen, resulting in the death of 42,000 men of Ephraim. Jephthah's vow cost him his only child and heir—a devastating sacrifice. Then there was a series of "judges" who took up leadership in Israel for various periods of time. The last one mentioned had forty sons and thirty grandsons who rode on seventy donkeys— quite a claim to fame, in fact the only one. Had wealth become the principle requirement for leadership? Is it today?

As we open Judges 13, we read that the Lord had given Israel into the hands of the Philistines. The Philistines directly oppressed Israel for a period of forty years with a strategy that produced cultural and spiritual assimilation and apathy. At the end there was no outcry, no cry to God for deliverance. Scripture simply tells us that God sent an angel to a barren woman to tell her she would have a son "who will begin to deliver Israel out of the hands of the Philistines (Judges 13:5)." Initial excitement over the possibility of that deliverer being a precursor of the Messiah is quickly dissolved. What was Manoah's response when his wife brought news of the angelic visitation and message? Unbelief, skepticism, confusion, unfamiliarity, and uncertainty all seem to be possible elements of his prayer asking God to send the Man of God again to teach them how to raise the promised child. Then, when God answered Manoah's prayer with a second visitation of the same messenger, we read that the question was answered, but there remained some obvious ignorance about the messenger, the required response, and the nature of God. All of this is evidence of not only a successful Philistine strategy, but also the generations of cultural and spiritual decline in Israel that preceded it.

Judges 14 introduces us to Samson, the boy foretold in the previous chapter, now an adult. The opening scenes with Samson choosing a Philistine woman to be his wife, then arguing with his parents about her, is troubling, to say the least. More confusing is the author's commentary in verse 4 that explains that the Philistine wife was to be part of God's strategy, providing an occasion to move against her people. The weapon was revealed to be Samson's supernatural strength. The account leaves us with more questions than answers. Why was Samson such a womanizer? Why the obnoxious riddles? Why the effective, almost serendipitous strategies? Why did Samson fight alone? This was a most unusual Divine plan of deliverance, was it not? In the end it appears that God used all of Samson's strengths, as well as his weaknesses, to begin the overthrow of an enemy that the nation seemed committed to placating—peace at any cost (see Judges 15:9—13). It would not be until the reign of King David that the Philistines were finally subdued.

The rest of the book of Judges shows us that the decline of the people of God continued. Judges 17:6 says, "In those days there was no king in Israel: every man did what was right in his own eyes." This same statement is repeated in the last verse of the book, Judges 21:25, with the five chapters between telling one woeful tale after another of in-fighting, deceptions, crime, and devastation. Israel did not need an outside oppressor to trouble them. The good news is that God was not finished with His people yet. The book of Ruth, which follows Judges, is a picture of true redemption. Additionally, it set up the line of David, out of which Jesus, our Messiah, came. The final Judge, Samuel, served in Israel after the book of Judges, through the anointing of Saul, then David, ushering in the age of the kingdom of Israel.

What Did Jesus Do?

Let's look at Jesus as Teacher through the lens of His third miracle in John 5:1—15. This account begins with a rather detailed description of the Pool of Bethesda. Think about why this might have been important to John in telling the story. What does it reveal about the mindset or beliefs of the people gathered there?

Do we have any such strong convictions about the sources, or means, of healing in our day? Think carefully!

Have you ever been curious about the large number of sick and invalid people at the Pool on the day Jesus visited? John does not tell us if Jesus healed any more than one. John 5:6 tells us that Jesus noticed a particular man among the crowd and perceived that he had been in his condition for a long time. How did Jesus approach him?

What was the man's response?

What is significant to you about the way Jesus healed the man in verse 8?

Is there any way in which Jesus withheld vital information for selfish purposes?

Did He hide His identity or manipulate the man to whom He ministered to create dependence or require homage? Did Jesus use deceptions as Samson had done? Remember what John records later in John 5, "I tell you the truth, the Son can do nothing by Himself; He can do only what He sees His Father doing, because whatever the Father does, the Son also does." At that point, Jesus defended the Sabbath miracle as the work of God, and His own teachings as the words of God. He was open with those who questioned Him despite the cost it would be to Him.

What was Jesus's final instruction to the man He healed?

John 19 provides an account of Jesus's sentencing and crucifixion. In it Jesus never exalts or defends Himself. He does not rail against His accusers. In fact, the only personal statement He made to people was, "I am thirsty." Those simple words connect us to His humanity and His vulnerability even while "God was in Christ reconciling the world to Himself (2 Corinthians 5:19, NKJV)." After His resurrection from death, Jesus testified that all authority in Heaven and earth has been given to Him, Matthew 28:19. The Father exalted the Son because Jesus never used the truth of who He was, or the power of that truth, to serve Himself or manipulate others to serve Him. His words are life. He is the Living Word.

Application Points

1. The <u>cause</u> for this curse coming upon Israel was her sin.
2. The <u>generational sins</u> that foster this curse are lying, deceiving, withholding, or otherwise manipulating truth in order to control people or circumstances for personal gain at the expense of others.
3. <u>Markers</u> of the Philistine curse: The principal marker of this curse is that you lack one key resource to progress in possessing your birthright, *i.e.* earn what you are "worth" in the market place. For Israel it was the knowledge of blacksmithing.
4. <u>Parallel redemptive gift</u>: Teaching, Romans 12:7, is the spiritual gift of imparting information in life-giving, empowering ways.

5. <u>Legitimacy lie</u>: I am legitimate when I have truth or information that gives me power. It is the unrighteous control of information to secure one's position, identity, or territory.

6. <u>Blessing</u>: When the Philistine curse has been broken we are able to enthrone Jesus in our lives and in our land. This keeps the devourers away and allows us to acquire all the pieces necessary to accomplish what God has planned for us to do (Ephesians 2:10).

Prayer of Renunciation and Cleansing

Almighty God and Heavenly Father, the earth is Yours and everything in it. I proclaim the truth that You created man in Your image and placed him in dominion as Your ambassador here. You are worthy of all worship, honor, and glory, all our strength, and obedience. You alone are God.

I confess that I, as well as all my ancestors before me, have failed miserably to enthrone You alone as Lord. Here and now I ask You, Father, to open the books of my family lines. I want to stand in the light. Expose all that is there that is sin that has opened the door for this Philistine curse. I reject and renounce the following:

- FEARS: of the future, of men, of present obstacles, of inadequacy, of powerlessness, of hurt and pain;
- All that has drawn us to seek power and control by manipulating knowledge/information;
- Using truth, power, and control to keep others in bondage;
- Seeing truth and/or knowledge as our legitimacy;
- Putting the enemy of our souls on the throne of our lives and in our land.

I agree for the breaking off of every dedication of land, social, and civic institutions and covenants made as part of those sinful behaviors.

I acknowledge that it was right and just for the Philistine curse to come into my family because of these sins. I also stand at the foot of the cross of Jesus Christ, admitting that there is a higher love and justice in His death and resurrection. You have all authority in heaven and earth, Jesus. Because of my confession, I claim the washing of my sin and these sins in my family lines, by the blood of the Lamb, as Your Word has promised (1 John 1:9).

Furthermore, I revoke the welcome of any spiritual demonic forces and powers associated with this curse and send all to the feet of Jesus.

Jesus, You are the Way, the Truth, and the Life. I rededicate myself to the Lord Jesus Christ alone, with Father and Holy Spirit, our triune God, Lord of the universe and all eternity, the only true God. Fill me with Your Spirit and lead me into Your freedom. Teach me to seek Your strategies and to steward all the resources You have entrusted to me so that life and freedom flow through me to others. Be enthroned upon the praises of all my generations, in our lives, and in the very land. In Jesus's glorious name, Amen.

CHAPTER 10
In Conclusion

From the very beginning, in the opening chapters of Genesis, to the breathtaking prophecies at the end of Revelation, the Scriptures make it clear that the Sovereign Creator has a plan. Each of us holds a piece of that plan in our very DNA. Genesis 1:26 is a declaration of God's purpose for mankind: "Let Us make man in Our image, according to Our likeness; let them have dominion…" To Adam and Eve God said, "Be fruitful and multiply; fill the earth and subdue it; Have dominion over" all life on the earth (Genesis 1: 28, NKJV). Then God showed them the provision He had made for sustenance and reproduction for all living plants, animals, fish, birds, and people. Fundamentally, God engineered birthright in the very beginning.

Those same words at the beginning of Genesis also serve to establish the mode of relationship with God: Covenant. Initially, the relationship between ELOHIM and Adam and Eve was open and free. Sin brought a break in relationship. Death entered the perfection God had made. Blood was shed so that God could provide coverings for Adam and Eve. They were evicted from Eden for their own protection, but God promised that He would one day reverse the reversal that sin had brought into the world. Another covenant. Over the centuries the Sovereign God has modified, added, and expanded covenants with mankind, in order to provide for the coming fulfillment of the Eternal Covenant. The Scriptures include covenants with Noah, Abraham, Moses, King David, and the New Covenant in Christ's blood, to name a few. In every one, God renews the original, most foundational promise: I will be your God and you will be my beloved people.

This study of Judges has had us looking at what happens when unrepentant sin corrupts the pathway of blessing God designed from generation to generation. The resulting consequences effect generational curses which have power to seriously compromise our ability to live out the birthright God intends. Let's review the generational sins, the curses they brought upon Israel, and the solution God has provided in Jesus Christ. Remember that the generational curses all manifest in the oppressors God engaged to discipline His covenant people, Israel.

Also significant is the recognition that all the curses arise out of the context of family.

Cushan-Rishathaim was the Aramean king who enslaved Israel for eight years (Judges 3:7—11). His very name means doubling of evil, indicative of a prior generation's alliance with evil, most likely through divination or witchcraft. In answer to Israel's repentance and cry for help, God raised up Othniel, a righteous man from a generational line of righteous men. Othniel's commission was to judge Israel and deliver them from the oppression and injustices of their slavery to Cushan-Rishathaim. We see this curse in us when witchcraft or rebellion in our generational lines works against us so that we cannot get justice, cannot earn what our labor is worth, or find power/empowerment to pursue our birthright. Breaking the curse through repentance, renunciation, and the appropriation of the Blood of Christ over that generational sin releases power to establish, or access, a proper legal system and justice. In Christ we receive the Holy Spirit and access to the place of intimacy with God, the Counsel of God, and the Court of Heaven. Also, the release of the gift of prophecy brings revelation to apply the power and solutions of heaven to our problems on earth.

The Moabites were the descendants of Lot and incestuous relations with his eldest daughter. The sin that violated moral and civil boundaries, and the sin of Lot's failure as a father to provide lawful means for future generations, were manifest generations later against Israel, in Judges 3:12—30. Lot's indulgences were mirrored in the Moabite King, Eglon. God's deliverer, Ehud, risked his own life to dispatch the king, whose pleasure Israel served. Then, Ehud led the army of Israel to retake control of her borders and strong cities. Breaking the Moabite curse allows us to establish healthy boundaries, keep what we have earned, and brings favor that helps create a platform from which we can pursue our birthright. Ehud's gift of service enabled Israel's independence from Moab.

The Canaanite curse, Judges 4 & 5, originated when Noah cursed Canaan for his father's, Ham's, dishonorable attempt to exploit Noah's shame. Exploitation, perversion, and harsh oppression were sins manifest in the generations of Canaan. When God sold Israel into the hand of the Canaanites, they terrorized Israel with 900 iron chariots, dominating the fertile farmlands and relegating displaced Israelites to a life of scraping by in hiding places and wilderness hillsides. Deborah was the judge God used to bring about Israel's liberation.

Breaking this curse frees us to develop the resources God has intended with time, provision, and godly leadership or mentors. Deborah's wisdom was evident in the gift of exhortation.

The Midianites who oppressed Israel in Judges 6:1—8:28 were descendants of a son of Abraham by a wife he took after Sarah's death. Abraham gave Midian and his brothers each a gift, then sent them away to the East as a protection for Isaac. The generational curse became one of devouring Israel's resources. God raised up Gideon, led him in small steps of faith, and with a small force of 300 men, vanquished a huge Midianite encampment. When the Midianite curse is broken off our family we will see resources begin to work for us, leveraging small investments for multiplication to the next generation. Though Abraham tried to bribe Midian and his brothers with a gift, the redemptive gift of giving actually strengthens and blesses for generations.

Judges 8:29—9:57 gives the account of Jotham's curse. Jotham, youngest son of Gideon, pronounced a curse against his illegitimate half-brother, Abimelech, and his allies, for violating covenant honor and gratitude toward their father, Gideon, as well as Jehovah, and for murdering his seventy brothers in order to make himself king in Israel. Abimelech was willing to destroy family in order to build his own kingdom. We experience Jotham's curse today when social structures are repeatedly destroyed from within by internal division. With division comes loss of strategic resources. God actually judged in Jotham's favor. Breaking this curse enables us to build social structures that are synergistically life-giving to the culture. Honor, and the gifts of godly leadership, are keys to this aspect of birthright.

By the time Jehovah sold Israel into the hands of the Ammonites, Judges 10—12, the generational sins in both societies had degraded them together. Ammon was the son of Lot and his younger daughter. Jephthah, in Judges, was an Israelite son of Gilead and a harlot, or concubine. The Ammonites worshipped Molech and instituted child sacrifice into their worship. When oppressing Israel, they crossed the borders and harassed and warred against them severely. Jephthah, outcast by the legitimate sons of his father, honed his skills as a valiant warrior across the border. When Jephthah was summoned back to Israel and offered a position of leadership, even receiving from Lord Jehovah a baptism of the Holy Spirit to enable victory over the Ammonites, he was unsure. In that uncertainty, Jephthah, like Lot's younger daughter, compromised; he made a vow of radical sacrifice which ultimately cost him his inheritance. Within the family covenant as God established it, there is a flow of love and mercy. Under the Ammonite curse one is unable to know this security, and so reaches to secure the love and favor of God through sacrifice. When this curse is broken we begin to perceive the glory of Jesus made manifest in His mercy to us, which then releases mercy to others. It is intimacy with God that enables us to supernaturally possess our birthright.

The Philistine curse, Judges 13—16, really seems to have arisen out of an illegitimate covenant between Abraham and King Abimelech of the Philistines. Because of this covenant, repeated by Isaac a generation later, as well as the Philistine rejection of Jehovah as God alone, it was many generations of oppression against Israel before they were finally subdued. (God honors our covenants more than we do!) Judges 13 details how God sovereignly caused a barren couple to conceive the son whom God would uniquely equip to begin the emancipation of Israel from the Philistines. Samson was an unusual weapon in every respect. He was God's answer to unlocking the manipulation and control of vital information the Philistines kept from Israel. When we experience the Philistine curse today it manifests as a perpetual lack of one vital piece of information, credential, or requirement that would free us to lay hold of our birthright. Release from the curse enables us to bring the blessing of Jesus's Lordship into the mountain of influence associated with that birthright, thereby enthroning Jesus in the land.

After doing business with these generational sins and curses in your life, you may well ask, where do I go from here? Breaking off the generational curses that have inhibited your ability to achieve your birthright is one very important part of a two-sided coin. The face of the coin represents the ways a person comes into agreement with those sins and curses, whether consciously or subconsciously. Romans 12:1—2, Hebrews 12:14, James 1:2—5, Philippians 3:12, and many other scriptures, direct us to engage with the Bible and the Holy Spirit for the transformation from carnality into Kingdom perspective by the renewing of our minds. We are to abide in Christ, know the truth, put on the armor of God, take thoughts captive, sow, and reap from the mind of Christ. It is a journey well worth the pursuit.

The End or The Beginning!

It is our ardent prayer that each student who perseveres to the end of this teaching will fully apprehend the life-giving freedoms encountered herein.

May the journey forward be lighter because the generational baggage has been let go.

May the future and hope to which we are called in Christ Jesus become an increasing reality in every facet of life.

May you come to fully possess your birthright, laying hold "of that for which God, in Christ Jesus, has laid hold of " you (Philippians 3:12).

"For it is for freedom that Christ has set us free (Galatians 5:1a, NIV)."

Doyle and Rebecca Musser

Endnotes

1. Kris Vallotton and Bill Johnson, *Supernatural Ways of Royalty* (PA: Destiny Image Publishers, Inc., 2006), 18

2. Jon & Jolene Hamil, *Crown & Throne* (Washington, D.C.: Burning Lamp Media & Publishing)

3. Johnny Enlow, *The Seven Mountain Prophecy*, (FL: Creation House, 2008), 193.

4. Op cit, page *xx*.

5. *Webster's Collegiate Dictionary* (NY: Random House Inc, 2000), "birthright"

6. Vallotton, 220

7. John Eldredge, *Wild at Heart,* (TN: Thomas Nelson Inc, 2001, 2010), 74.

8. William and Janet Sudduth, *5 Types of Curses,* DVD, (CO: Righteous Acts Ministries).

9. Enlow, 43.

10. Ibid. 97.

11. Hamil, *xxii*.

12. Op cit, 44.

13. Abraham Lincoln, *The Gettysburg Address and Other Writings, a compilation*, (NY: Fall River Press, 2010), 151.

14. Tony Evans, PhD, *The Power of God's Names*, (OR: Harvest House Publishers, 2014), 123.

15. *Webster's*, "tribute".

16. Ibid, "exhortation".

17. Evans, 108.

18. Op cit, "raven"

19. G. Douglas Young, editor, *Young's Compact Bible Dictionary,* (IL: Tyndale House Publishers Inc., 1984), "zeba".

20. Ibid, "zalmunna".

21. *Webster's*, "ruler, noun".

22. Ibid, "rule, verb".

23. ibid, "lead, verb".

24. R. Russell Bixler, *Commentary: New Spirit Filled Life Bible, NKJV,* (TN: Nelson, 2002), 30.

25. op cit, "teach, *noun, verb*".

Selected Bibliography

Bevere, John. *The Bait of Satan*. FL: Charisma House, 1994.

Brown, Rebecca and Yoder, Daniel. *Unbroken Curses*. PA: Whitaker House, 1995.

Burk, Arthur. *The Seven Curses on Your Finances*. CA: Plumbline Ministries, 2004.

Conner, Kevin J. and Malmin, Ken. *The Covenants: The Key to God's Relationships with Mankind*. OR: City Bible Publishing, 1983, 1997.

Eldredge, John. *Wild at Heart: Discovering the Secret of a Man's Soul*. TN: Thomas Nelson Inc, 2001, 2010.

Enlow, Johnny. *The Seven Mountain Prophecy*. FL: Creation House, 2008.

Evans, Dr. Tony. *The Power of God's Names*. OR: Harvest House Publishers, 2014.

Gross, Chester. *The Covenants*. WA: CreateSpace Independent Publishing, 2014.

Hamil, Jon & Jolene. *Crown & Throne*. Washington, D.C.: Burning Lamp Media and Publishing, 2013.

Hayford, Jack W., executive editor, *New Spirit Filled Life Bible, NKJV*. TN: Thomas Nelson Bibles, 2002.

Henderson, Robert. *Operating in the Court of Heaven*. TX: Robert Henderson Ministries, 2016.

Lincoln, Abraham. *The Gettysburg Address and Other Writings, a compilation*. NY: Fall River Press, 2010.

Sudduth, William & Janet, *"5 Types of Curses"* DVD, CO: Righteous Acts Ministries.

Vallotton, Kris and Johnson, Bill. *Supernatural Ways of Royalty*. PA: Destiny Image Publishers, Inc, 2006.

Webster's Collegiate Dictionary. NY: Random House Inc, 2000.

Wood, Leon. *Distressing Days of the Judges*. MI: Zondervan Publishing House, 1975, 1980.

Young, G. Douglas, PhD., *Young's Compact Bible Dictionary*. IL: Tyndale House Publishers Inc, 1984.

Printed in the United States
by Baker & Taylor Publisher Services